# HEAL
## to
# LEAD

KELLY L. CAMPBELL

# HEAL to LEAD

### Revolutionizing Leadership through Trauma Healing

WILEY

For general information on our other products and services or for technical support, please contact our Customer Care Department within the United States at (800) 762-2974, outside the United States at (317) 572-3993 or fax (317) 572-4002.

Wiley also publishes its books in a variety of electronic formats. Some content that appears in print may not be available in electronic formats. For more information about Wiley products, visit our web site at www.wiley.com.

*Library of Congress Cataloging-in-Publication Data is Available:*

ISBN: 978-1-394-21315-3 (cloth)
ISBN: 978-1-394-21316-0 (ePub)
ISBN: 978-1-394-21317-7 (ePDF)

COVER DESIGN: PAUL MCCARTHY
COVER ART: © GETTY IMAGES | JAMIELAWTON

SKY10071171_033124

*For my grandmother, Ann, who taught me the wisdom of innate leadership*

# Contents

# Prologue

INTUITIVELY, I CAN sense their approach, and in the distant sky, I hear the unmistakable calls on the wind. The sounds in unison turn a smile on my face, as if each muscle is engaged in the effortlessness of my joy. My grandmother has sent another flock of geese to soar overhead. For more than 20 years since her passing, this is her loving gesture to remind me to lift my gaze, feel the fullness of universal synchronicity, and remember.

My grandmother loved Canada geese more than anyone I've ever met. She was awestruck by the innate wisdom of these birds to rotate leaders based on how well rested they were. Exactly how they make the decision to swap, scientists do not know, but what they have discovered is that by flying in a V formation, a flock increases its flight range by about 71%. As a result, each of the birds exerts far less energy and can glide more often.[1] The birds at the back honk at those up front as a means of encouragement to keep a consistent pace. If a single goose falls out of formation, it immediately experiences the resistance that comes with flying alone. Realizing the impossibility of sustaining a solo journey, it quickly returns to the advantage of the gaggle's streamlined, uplifting power. When a member of the flock falls away due to illness or injury, two others join its journey as a means of protection and care until the goose either recovers or perishes. Then the two or three of them join a new flock, and the cycle of regenerative leadership continues.

My grandmother honored nature for its intelligent design and beauty. Her influence on my life and life's work has been profound, more so than I had realized before writing *Heal to Lead*. In particular, her astute recognition of *innate leadership* seeped into my psyche from a young age through some osmotic phenomenon: the most effective leader is not the loudest nor the one who desires the credit, but the one who knows the importance of caring for others and who believes in the regenerative power of the collective.

In *Braiding Sweetgrass*, author Robin Wall Kimmerer shares the Native American story of how North America, or Turtle Island, was formed after Skywoman's fall from above was broken by the rising of warm, softly feathered wings. Her recount reminds us all of *the generosity of geese*.[2] There is so much compassion and wisdom held within their wings, and yet in the colonial loss of reverence for the natural world and humankind, there has been a mass migration toward disintegration—what has incorrectly become understood as *leadership*.

Somewhere along the way, modern man assumed he could outsmart Mother Nature. In silencing intuition and devaluing natural fluency for the last 500 years, we have all been paying the price. Today, the cost of status quo continuance has been made exponentially higher because modern leadership choices have prioritized short-term progress to our peril, relegating most of us to suffer.

The norms of so-called leadership have meant going it alone, flying until we're burnt out, honking at those behind us, allowing unsupported members to fall away, and neglecting our universal community. It's easy to name all the reasons why change cannot be made because quieting our inner wisdom also blocks our ingenuity and willingness. As high-conscious leaders, though, it is possible to revert to our inherent goodness and change course completely. Where we can begin is within our control; the starting point just happens to be what most of us have been avoiding until now.

You and I were born whole, intrinsically good-hearted, and with an ability to distinguish kindness from cruelty. Our experiences of the traumatic events that have happened to us have incrementally shielded us from the profoundness of our kind, loving nature. The discomfort we all feel, to some degree, is due to that stark contrast between how we came into this world and who we are now. But we do not have to proceed disconnected from a central flow of life force. We do not have to destroy each other and the land under our feet in the name of greed, God, status, or power. This is not who we are. We know better but we have forgotten much. There is another way.

Within each of us lies the gateway to healing ourselves, trusting each other, and honoring the gifts of the world we inhabit. By working through our own trauma, we can re-form the shape of leadership and return to a higher state of consciousness.

# Introduction

SITTING IN THE back seat of the family car, a white Crown Victoria with velvety, navy blue interior, my younger brother next to me, my mother pulled into the parking lot of the shopping plaza where our local movie theater was located. She maneuvered the gear shift into park, slung her right arm over the passenger seat, and turned around to look at us. "I wanted to let you know that your father won't be living with us for a while. He has some things to work out. And I don't know when he'll be back. . . . So, are you ready to see *Honey, I Shrunk the Kids?*"

Talk about shrinking already small children. Even at nine years old, I knew their marriage was rocky, but the words streaming from her mouth didn't make sense. I had so many questions. So many emotions. Mostly, fear. Who would protect me from her if he was gone from our house? I recall a distinct disconnect between her words and demeanor. No mutual responsibility taken for their dysfunctional relationship, no modicum of reassurance that everything would be okay, no time or safe space offered for Q&A. And now she wanted us to sit through some comedic science fiction movie?

I looked over at Kevin, just a year younger—Irish twins, as they say—a distinct mix of shock in his body and tears already starting to stream down his face, lip quivering. Within seconds, I tried to fit all of the pieces into the compartments that my logical brain could comprehend, organize the disparities, and suppress any emotions that were trying to make themselves known. I put my hand on my eight-year-old brother's back and then wrapped my arm around his shoulder. I watched his face, a mirror to my own experience. I leaned in to console him the only way I knew how in that moment and said, "It's gonna be okay, bud."

More than anything, I wanted someone to hold me. To explain what was actually happening, what I should expect. I needed someone to reassure me that I would not be in more danger. It was clear that she wasn't going to do anything to assuage either of us except pretend that the distraction of a kid's movie would somehow make it all seem normal.

Of course I couldn't concentrate. The concept of the movie seemed disjointed, much like the way she communicated this life-altering news and then ushered us to our sticky theater seats. I kept looking over to see how Kevin was holding up. He was in pain but distracting himself with laughter and candy as a means of emotional protection. I don't remember anything about the ride home except my brother's whispered question, "Do you think we'll ever see dad again?" My heart broke inside the walls of my small chest. "Yeah, totally. He'll come see us all the time. I know he will. I promise."

I was afraid of and angry at my mother simultaneously, but I had become adept at compartmentalizing my feelings, too. I was able to quell my brother's worries and make everything feel a little less scary, even if just for the night. It was the first time I recall exhibiting *courage*, in that I could assess a difficult situation and, despite my own fear and uncertainty, open my heart to support someone who needed guidance. I didn't know it at the time, but my leadership abilities were being inadvertently honed day by day throughout my childhood.

When I was asked the singular question that would spur the direction of this book—"*What was the first moment in your life that you remember stepping into a leadership role?*"—I was caught entirely off guard by the memory of sitting in that car. I expected that my mind would conjure recollections of high school volleyball or softball team captainship, or of hiring my first employee as a young business owner. I hadn't realized that this latent memory was living in my body. I hadn't recounted that event even once since the night in that parking lot. It spoke to something greater that was still unhealed in me. Even after a decade and a half of talk therapy, I couldn't shake the deep knowing that I was still carrying a lot of past trauma.

Childhood experiences, in which we weren't made to feel safe, valued, loved, or a sense of belonging, impact us to such depths that our coping mechanisms become the foundation for how we view the world and our place within it. They impact how we interact with others when we're young as much as what we choose to prioritize later in life.

Over the last few years, I have come to understand what trauma actually is: *information that is unprocessed, or unintegrated, within the psyche and in the body.* Trauma is not who we are. It is not our identity. Trauma is not something to be ashamed of, nor were the things we experienced our fault. We did nothing to invite, attract, or provoke those negative encounters. It's important to understand, right from the beginning of this book, that in our own experiencing of negative events, we were on the receiving end of someone else's unprocessed pain. When we don't do the work of healing our wounds, we perpetuate a harmful cycle.

In the context of leadership, trauma can manifest as a spectrum of behaviors that range from people controlling to people pleasing. Examples might include dominance, expectation of perfection, and micromanaging. Or, on the flip side, overgiving, having poor boundaries, and dissociating. The underlying belief running through both is that we are damaged—and therefore unworthy of being accepted simply for who we are. How detrimental it is to us and others when our wounds drive our leadership style.

Regardless of your brand of traumatic experiences, none of us escaped our formative years unscathed. Each of us has our own version of *not being enough.* That's because acts of survival in early life determine many of our ideologies as adults about love and belonging: how it looks or sounds or feels, and how to abandon ourselves in order to receive it. We all have emotional wounds that have imprinted and fueled our strategies, actions, and belief systems as we mature. Hopefully, we will spend a lifetime trying to re-parent and reconnect with our own inner child to let that little version of us know that it's not only okay but in fact necessary to start communicating our needs and boundaries as adults—especially when those reflect what we did not receive during our youngest years.

Our primary parental relationships are what we rely upon for safety and external validation of the self—until we grow older and can provide that for ourselves. When we begin to revisit the scenes and memories from our past, we can see clearly how many of us were not given what we needed to flourish into healthy adults, let alone leaders. But here's the thing: *we cannot be the kind of leaders that our changing world needs and bypass the healing of psychological wounds from our past.*

Healing starts with introspection about the very experiences that have made us who we are as leaders today. These impact what we believe, why we think, speak, and behave the way we do, and how we show up as our true selves, or wear the mask that will simply help us assimilate. To experience personal growth and the becoming of a *high-conscious leader*, my experience is that the process entails deconstruction of your worldview and much of what you know about this current version of yourself. Sounds fun, right? Sign me up!

To become the kind of leader we need at this very moment—as we move forward in the new iteration of the world we're creating—there is an unraveling that is both natural and necessary. It's the molting of a skin that used to (or might still) feel uncomfortable to us as adults. It's learning how to regulate emotions, not by pushing them away, but by inviting them in, experiencing them, and then releasing historical attachment to them. It's acceptance of the fact that who you were, from an egoic sense, will need to die in order to be rebirthed as the leader those in your family, community, organization, and the world want to emulate.

Researcher and author Brené Brown's definition of a leader has resonated with me since *Dare to Lead* was published in 2018: "A leader is anyone who takes responsibility for finding the potential in people and processes, and who has the courage to develop that potential."[1] Yet we can't get to a place of taking responsibility, raising others up, or being courageous without first engaging in the process of healing ourselves.

Out of the four that I share throughout this book, perhaps *Integrating Trauma* is the most important fundamental of influential leadership. Healing begins by releasing old narratives about who we were, in favor of who we might be. In doing so, we get ever closer to the true nature of who we are as high-conscious leaders within or at the helm of our organizations: generous, kind and supportive, vulnerable and wise, curious, interested in those under our care surpassing any legacy we might leave, and restoration of being in right relationship with nature.

> *"Letting go is the path to freedom. It is only by letting go of the hopes, the fears, the pain, the past, the stories that have a hold on us that we can quiet our mind and open our heart."*[2]

**—Jack Kornfield**
*AUTHOR AND BUDDHIST MONK*

With all of the disruption and intense anxiety, leadership and learning demand more wisdom.

The frameworks that allow for wise healing are often counterintuitive to what has historically been valued in our culture. *More being and less doing* is antithetical to every message we've received to date. Keep that in mind as we take this journey together because there might be some discomfort, confusion, and resistance as you read. In fact, transformation without those experiences would be impossible.

And while transformation never takes the same form for any two people, here's a sense of what you can expect in the pages ahead. In Part I: Kintsukuroi, I explain why now is the time to lead more effectively. Part II: Preparing for the Journey is an exploration of what we mean by trauma, how trauma integration modalities are differentiated from mental health maintenance, what I mean by *high-conscious leadership*, and an outline of the four fundamentals thereof. Part III: When the Past Is Present dives head-first into trauma integration as the foundation for all else, including access to an online menu of healing modalities to give you a taste of what's available. Throughout this part, I share the personal stories of how trauma not only influenced who I am, but how I've been integrating my core wounding. In Part IV: True Strength, I make the case for the embodiment of vulnerability as the second fundamental for high-conscious leadership. I take that a step further by diving into the gift of failure, impostor syndrome, and upper limiting— some of the most vulnerable places for the egos of leaders. In Part V, Care in Action, I unpack the three different types of empathy, offer examples of how to use compassionate intelligence, and explain why a shift in intention—from productivity to employee well-being—is a guarantee for long-term organizational success. Finally, Part VI: The Great Remembering says that when we actively heal, we naturally want to light the way for others and contribute meaningfully in the world.

You might be feeling an inner lack of purpose, impact, or belonging. You're likely still reeling from all that has happened since 2020, including the governmental decisions to revoke many of our basic human rights in the United States—from reproductive justice,[3] access to a healthy environment, LGBTQIA+ rights, and gender-affirming care, to open discussion about critical race theory, gender identity, and social and land justice. Perhaps the introspection that was born of isolation and what we're confronting right now has sparked the feeling in you that *there has to be a better way to be in the world.*

Regardless of how *Heal to Lead* found its way to you, you've opened it because you're ready to go deeper. You're ready to discover a different perspective, to surrender, and to live a fulfilled life—for yourself and for the benefit of all stakeholders under your care. I'm rooting for you to find the purpose, stability, deep contentment, and natural joy you've been seeking for so long. Through sharing my healing leader's story, I want you to consider how yours has been in the making since you were a child. It feels like it's being called to the surface, too. Through these pages, you'll discover how your early experiences have shaped everything about you. As you begin to look within yourself, I ask only that you dial up your curiosity and reflect on the questions sprinkled throughout the following chapters.

I am unapologetic about my belief that we need to both deepen and widen our understanding of what's required for *real leadership.* That means owning our own trauma, healing the earth, and creating cultures in which our people feel safe, seen, heard, respected, valued, and included by default—not as an afterthought or a means of box-checking.

Can you imagine what would happen if we replaced command-and-control power, rigidity, and egocentricity with consciousness, collaboration, and genuine care for those under our stewardship? If the opposite of shrinking is expanding, doesn't that mean healing to lead in a soul-forward way so that we can all rise together? If the new hallmarks of effective leadership are self-development, empathy, vulnerability, honesty, and conscious communication, how can we lead organizations now and into a just future if we have not set our own foundation?

Within these questions lies a gap—the chasm between processing our past and bringing a higher level of consciousness to leadership. Up until this point, we have not named the profound space that exists between these two seemingly disparate pieces of ourselves as leaders. Why not?

- For starters, being open about trauma requires vulnerability, which has historically been viewed as a weakness by leaders.
- Mental health and psychological wounds have been stigmatized in society for centuries, and within most of America's workplaces, that stigma is even stronger.
- Thoughtfully processing inner information does not happen quickly, and it goes against our natural ability to discern the difference between threat to our survival and threat to our ego. Plus, most of us would prefer to do literally anything else.

This is brand new territory for many. As an on-ramp, what I can offer is a new set of four essentials for becoming an effective, high-conscious leader. Ultimately, you're the only one who can do the work though. By the end of this book, you might begin to see your own unhealed aspects. You might become curious about how to move toward emotional liberation and a more conscious approach to leading. Go slowly. If you can begin to do the transformative inner work that's required, I will show you that to lead effectively you must encounter the edges and depths of yourself.

I want to be clear that I do not have the answers that you will be searching for throughout this journey. Spoiler alert: you are whole and complete, and you are the subject matter expert of your own life. What I do have to share is a lived experience as a gender-fluid, social entrepreneur who is continuously healing and awakening, training and years of experience as a trauma-informed leadership coach and conscious leadership consultant, and imperatives to share as a series of mile markers. These are set up intentionally through a lens of axiology—shining a light on intrinsic, extrinsic, and systemic considerations. As you unpack your past, I'm game to be your guide so that you have a sense of the terrain that might lie ahead for you. Let's turn this page together.

# PART

# I

# Kintsukuroi

"*Keep looking at the bandaged place. That is where the light enters you.*"[1]
—*Jalāl al-Dīn Rumi*
*13th-CENTURY POET AND SUFI MYSTIC*

IN JAPANESE CULTURE, the concept of finding beauty in every aspect of imperfection in nature is referred to as *wabi-sabi*. It comes from the Buddhist teaching of the three basic truths of existence, in which we can think of all things as *imperfect, impermanent,* and *incomplete.* Wabi-sabi rails against the Western association between beauty and perfection, and it allows us to embrace the natural essence of being.

One of my favorite examples is *kintsukuroi*, the 400-year-old artful practice of mending broken pottery with liquid gold in order to honor the history and utility of breaks in the form. A metaphor for healing our own wounds, the process and visibility of repair actually creates something stronger, unique, and more approachable than the original. These cracks, or imperfections, show up in our leadership style.

Whether or not we choose to mend them determines the quality with which we lead others. Those who lead from a fear-based place of scarcity might be aggressive or passive-aggressive, dominant, demeaning, or micromanaging. Leaders who did not feel valued or worthy during childhood might unconsciously devalue those within

1

their organization. If they feel the need to prove their own worth, they might take credit for other people's ideas or work. They might never ask for input from their teams because they believe that they need to have all of the answers to gain respect.

I call these *low-conscious leaders*, and there is nothing inherently wrong with them. You might even resonate with one or more of these behaviors; I certainly did. Yet the light of awakening finds its way in somehow. Like a cracked clay vessel, all leaders are whole—and most are in need of healing to meet their highest function. There is a plethora of gold in the process of integrating one's trauma, as opposed to resisting the remedy or pretending those emotional wounds do not exist.

The gold emerges in moments of recognition when something deeper is activated, but you respond with intention—instead of reacting without any. You find yourself considering the impact that your decisions might have on all stakeholders. You develop a genuine curiosity for how others experience the world and feel compelled to act if someone needs support. Your ability to communicate more thoughtfully with your employees, clients, significant other(s), and children makes you feel proud. When you look back, a sense of wonder invites you to question how you lived any other way.

In the same way that our imperfections create a life that is rich, resilient, and abundant, the wounds we experience in childhood can one day break us open to the truth and the light of who we are as leaders.

# 1

## Why We Become Leaders

COURAGE—FROM THE LATIN *cor*, meaning *heart*—is herculean in the face of fear. The news that my dad was leaving us was heartbreaking for me. I wouldn't let anyone see or know that though. Not my mother. Not Kevin. Certainly not my dad; he was my advocate. I had already been people-pleasing for years up to this point, but now I was in a desperate position. Sure, I could have voiced how I felt to my father, but I sensed the gravity of the situation, and my survival strategy was to limit any risk in burdening or displeasing him. My future leadership tendency toward pleasing started right here, with this very experience. In my nine-year-old subconscious mind, I couldn't risk losing his love or protection because then I would be alone, with her, and in real danger.

In my heart though, I was disappointed and scared. I was angry at him, too, but I never let myself feel those emotions at the time. They didn't feel like safe emotions to have, so I stuffed them down like I had been doing with my mother all along. They piled up and calcified in my gut, but I pretended everything was fine between him and me. In fact, I put my father on a pedestal because any other subconscious strategy would have meant that both of my caregivers—the totality of my environment—were flawed and therefore unsafe.

More than 30 years later, I have come to realize that he knew my mother better than anyone. He knew what she was capable of, and he knew what was happening in our home. Maybe he was in some amount of denial and emotional repression due to his own experience with childhood physical abuse at the hands of his stepfather. To rescue me from our home would have forced him to engage with his own experience of abuse, and he was unable or unwilling. Relatedly, maybe his own gender-bias—that only men can exhibit violence and aggression to that extent—caused a blind spot for him. And whether either of these is true, I have come to trust that my feelings at nine were entirely valid. I love my dad, and he is fallible just like every one of us.

It wasn't until recently that two epiphanies emerged. First, I want a closer, more connected relationship with my father, but his capacity to engage with his own emotions keeps us in a relational dance that is loving and mostly utilitarian. We banter when we debate a topic, but his nature is reactionary and his default is to sarcasm. More often than not, he's listening to reply—not listening to understand. His wounds don't allow him the space to see what's important to me in a conversation, why I might place such value on the ideals I hold, or what emotion might be underneath what I'm saying. Though he has been the leader of our family, I had never viewed my father through the lens of his own trauma—until now. The depth of his heart is easy to observe, as is his unending generosity; I wonder if watching him is where I first learned that caring for others and being generous with time or resources are a subconscious, strategic duo that also help one gain love and belonging. Like any little boy, he just wanted to feel safe, loved, and appreciated within his family dynamic. I see that play out between us now that I'm in my 40s. And though I can get frustrated by our opposing communication styles, I remind myself of the root of his reactions. Few things would bring me greater joy than for my dad to integrate the traumatic experiences he has endured, but his choices are not my responsibility. I have realized that my nine-year-old self clung anxiously to the relationship because my life literally depended on it, and I've done a lot of work to unravel my insecure attachment style over the last three decades.

Secondly, all that said, I just might be more grateful for him today than ever before. He chose to break the patriarchal cycle of physical abuse within his own family and lineage, and he validated my experiences, no matter how difficult it might have been for him to recall being in my shoes.

One spring morning in 2021, I came across a podcast episode of Tom Bilyue's *Impact Theory* entitled, "Dr. Gabor Maté on How We Become Who We Are."[1] Dr. Maté is a Hungarian Canadian physician, best-selling author, and world-renowned expert on childhood development and trauma. Less than 15 minutes into the conversation, I realized why my father played such a large role in saving my life as a kid. He showed me kindness, was empathetic, and validated some of my most violent experiences with my mother. During the episode, Dr. Maté explained that many factors help determine resilience—and the greatest one of all is having just one person in your life who provides even a modicum of validation during childhood. I had two: my father and his mother, Ann.

Back then, my father's way of being unconsciously signaled to me that I might be loveable. *Maybe I'm not worthless. Maybe I do matter.* As a kid, all I needed was a miniscule hole to be poked in the story that I was broken and irreparably damaged. Physical abuse has a way of destroying the magic we come into this world with. I longed for something to counter what was being messaged to me daily by my mother, and my dad's validating words and actions created the possibility for me to become a healthy human. He is one reason why I did the work to remember who I am.

Dr. Maté went on to explain that there are two views each of us can choose from during our traumatic, formative years. We can either believe that there is something foundationally wrong with the world and our caretakers within it, or we can surmise that we must be the broken thing. The former view is much scarier, he says—because *if the environment is flawed, how can we ever feel safe in it?*

## Being Needed Versus Being Wanted

In the documentary *The Wisdom of Trauma*, Dr. Maté tells a personal and vulnerable story about not feeling wanted as a child. In feeling *unwanted*, he chose to become a medical doctor so that he would feel *needed* by his patients. His work in uncovering his own trauma led him to realize how much it plays a role in the positions we gravitate toward as adults.[2]

Many of us become leaders for one of three subconscious reasons:

1. We need to feel valued or prove ourselves worthy.
2. We need to dissociate from feelings of deep shame and powerlessness.
3. We feel a profound sense of responsibility for others.

When I put my arm around my brother the night my mother told us that my dad was leaving, I was making myself needed as much as I felt responsible to support him. As trauma survivors, we "value being needed because [we] can't imagine being wanted."[3] Many of us become leaders because we believe that if we can succeed, we'll prove to ourselves and everyone else that we have inherent worth.

## Shadow Leadership Styles

Trauma can both encourage us to be our best and, at the same time, hold us back from living and leading with higher consciousness. Some people fight their way to the top because their ego needs to protect itself by dominating others. Others cater to the whims of those under them out of fear of abandonment or rejection. We constantly play out our responses to early unmet needs. In other words, many of us who find ourselves in leadership positions are actually attempting to combat or distract ourselves from unresolved trauma.

Let's talk about what kind of leader you've become. To keep things simple, I've broken this down into just two trauma-based styles: *People Controllers* and *People Pleasers*. Across these two categories, the need to feel valued and worthy is foundational because it is a basic psychological need of all humans, regardless of the specific type or longevity of trauma. Some of my work is influenced by *Positive Intelligence*—the work of Shirzad Charmine, a Stanford lecturer leading research on the saboteurs we encounter within ourselves and how they can undermine our leadership efficacy.

## People Controllers

When perfectionism is taken to the extreme, it serves as temporary relief for People Controllers. The combination of self-doubt and fear of being judged by others is somehow quelled by doing things the right way, on time, without a single mistake or misstep. This sets up People Controllers for failure because perfection is an impossibility for themselves and for others.

Most controlling leaders don't understand that leadership is about influence more than anything else. The control mechanisms used are an attempt to avoid the deep shame and powerlessness they experienced in childhood. According to Shirzad Chamine, they "might have generated a sense of order in the middle of a chaotic family dynamic, or earned acceptance and attention from emotionally distant or demanding parents by standing out as the irreproachable, perfect kid."[4]

People-controlling leaders tend to micromanage, which erodes the empowerment of others. They assume they are always right, and that those within their organization approve of how they lead. They must have the final word in every decision and are deeply uncomfortable with any perceived threat to their authority. This is also referred to as *autocratic leadership.*

Archetypes include the Patriarch, the Hero, and the Dictator. Anyone who views themselves as a protector, breadwinner, authoritarian, or disciplinarian would likely fall into this category. If they had integrated their past trauma, they would recognize that they can only control their own reactions, attitudes, and biases—never people or other external forces.

*"To empower people means learning how to lead people without controlling them."*[5]

**—Dave Kraft**
*MISTAKES LEADERS MAKE*

## People Pleasers

According to Beatrice Chestnut, people-pleasing leaders unconsciously strive to be liked by as many people as possible. They attempt to earn attention and acceptance through helping, rescuing, or flattering others. An underlying fear of rejection stems from childhood trauma and shows up as conflict avoidance, burnout due to inability to delegate, selflessness, poor boundaries, dependence, and even manipulation.[6]

People-pleasers are naturally empathetic, supportive, positive, and thrive in connection and meaningful relationships. However, the shadow traits here are actually self-serving, in that their ability to read and interpret the facial expressions, body language, and tonality of others provides all the information they need to position themselves well for being seen as genuine and caring. This can stray strongly off course when others don't notice or seem to care what their people-pleasing leader has done for them. They might become resentful, believing others are selfish and unappreciative—although they would never express those sentiments for fear of rejection or loss of relationship. They struggle to give and receive feedback, and they have difficulty holding others accountable.

Archetypes include the Matriarch, the Martyr, and the Peacemaker. Anyone who views themselves as a caretaker, rescuer, or cheerleader likely falls into this category. Ultimately, People Pleasers are no more effective at leadership than People Controllers. If they had integrated their childhood wounds, they would lead with compassionate empathy and healthy boundaries, address challenges using conscious communication, and prioritize their well-being by trusting others with delegated responsibilities.

When I look at my own upbringing and traumatic relationship with my mother, I see why I chose to make the courageous leap into starting a business at such a young age. I didn't feel worthy or loved by her, so I created a reality in which I would be needed by my employees and clients. It was just as important to prove to the world that I was valuable as it was to prove that to her and to myself.

To use Chamine's explanation about the *original survival function* of pleasers like me: two assumptions absorbed during childhood feed their worldview:

1. I must put others' needs ahead of my own.

2. I must give love and affection in order to get any back. I must earn [love because I am] not simply worthy of it.[7]

Taking that a step further, I wanted to be the kind of matriarch who showed up as the antithesis of my mother; I cared deeply about my team and our roster of clients. I know I allowed some to take advantage of my people-pleasing tendencies, and I avoided letting a few employees go for longer than I should have. My leadership evolution aligned with my personal values, but I was also proving to myself that I was nothing like my mother. That I was kind and good and caring. Beneficial and likable in the world.

Clearly, I tended toward people pleasing, but there are aspects of each shadow leadership style with which I identify. In fact, as the young owner of a cause marketing agency, I'm sure I shifted from one to the other of these categories, depending on what I had to manage on any given day. And while I repeated a behavioral pattern to ensure my unmet psychological needs were fulfilled, I do know that I did the best I could with the tools I had at the time.

## Sorting for Sanity

My mother displayed characteristics of both Narcissistic and Borderline Personality Disorders (NPD and BPD), and the brand of love she was able to give didn't feel like love at all. I did not understand this at the time, but my mother saw me as the small version of herself, whom she loathed. She viewed me as competition for my father's attention and affection, as if there was a finite amount to go around. She took every opportunity to hurt me and keep me small. Nothing I did could ever be enough for her to love me the way most mothers love their children. The physical abuse I endured, in many ways, was easier to heal from than its verbal and emotional counterparts.

To survive within that environment, I relied on a subconscious categorization system to decipher her actions and words. I developed strategies and methods to organize, in my mind, the complex information I was continuously gathering. Understanding patterns or cues made me feel like I could better predict shifts in her moods to keep myself safe. Of course, I didn't know I was doing this at the time, but it became clear as I was writing this book that I was employing a brilliant filtration method as a kid, placing my experiences in four mental receptacles:

1. **I trust myself:** *"That's not right. Something is definitely off about her."*
2. **I can't be sure what's true:** *"Did that really happen? Is that believable?"*
3. **I have to work harder:** *"I'll get it perfect next time; maybe then she'll love me."*
4. **I am unlovable:** *"She's right; I must be bad, damaged, or irreparably broken."*

These receptacles were like bins for garbage, compost, and recycling paper and plastic. In considering each behavior or hurtful phrase, I was scrutinizing its validity. *How do I digest this? Do I agree to receive this, and if so, how? Where does this live, based on how true it is?* Being on the receiving end of someone with BPD and NPD can make you feel unstable, and I believe this intuitively invented system was another piece of what saved my life. This was less about developing self-awareness early on; rather, it was a vital way to sort for my own sanity.

Luckily, for some reason, most of the inputs fell into the first receptacle and the rest were split among the latter three. What fell into the last two, though, embedded themselves deeply into adulthood, impacting nearly every relationship in my life. My need to earn love, protect myself from rejection, and validate my sense of self built the wobbly foundation of my leadership story. I invite you to pause here and consider any of your own experiences from childhood that might be similar, where your primary caregivers or other adults in your life said things or behaved in ways that hurt you—and forced you to consider whether they were actually true.

What frameworks, systems, or methods might you have invented during childhood?

Do you think they might still be influencing your thought processes today, as an adult?

## Survival Superpowers

It makes sense that I became a keen witness. Through the power of observation, I noticed everything that was said and went unsaid in our home, from facial expressions and body language to energetic shifts in the room. Skills like these help us survive our younger years. They protect our developing ego. They help us learn how to resource when lack creates friction in unmet needs. We create frameworks for the things that we might come to realize later in life were a goddamn gift.

Until one day, they're not. One day, you understand that there are mechanisms that no longer serve you, personally and professionally. They might actually be the very things that hold you back from becoming who you are meant to be—before someone told you who you were. Before someone forced you to shrink into a smaller version of yourself.

These frameworks are life-saving, even life-giving, so the idea that you would purposefully destroy them seems unwise. But the reality is that there's a whole world of emotional regulation, effective communication, radical self-love, and joy available to you if you can take the courageous step to tear it all down. This level of realization and self-awareness comes at an emotional cost, but that cost is also a necessary release. Up to this point, you might have been repressing so much emotion that it's difficult for you to decipher how your way of being is no longer serving you. If you listen to the voice within and pay attention to the sensation in your body, you know there's a different way. You can feel that something better is waiting on the other side of something. I understand how it can all feel so uncertain, so vague. You have no idea what that something is or how long it might take to arrive.

What I can share is that I was so used to feeling victimized that I discounted the notion that I could choose a different path. I was so used to talking about what my mother had done to me that I forgot I could start focusing on the future instead of living in the past. I had a choice in the matter of who I could become—as a person, a partner, and a leader.

Though I want to say that I became a leader accidentally, nothing about my journey thus far has been coincidental. The truth is that I became a leader because it was necessary for me to rewrite my personal narrative. I needed to experience the trials and tribulations of business ownership, employee attrition, over-servicing clients, finding my voice, enacting healthy boundaries, losing relationships, and creating a generative path forward for myself.

Why do you think you became a leader?

# 2

---

# Low-Conscious Leaders
# Are Everywhere

WOUNDED LEADERS ARE easy to spot, aren't they? In business, they lead with fear-based tactics like dominance, aggression, and rigidity. In politics, they succumb to the interests of a few despite detrimental impact to the whole. Low-conscious leaders make decisions without any input from the collective above which they find themselves perched—or worse, they ask for input and decide against the majority anyway. They take credit for other people's ideas. They prefer to keep others feeling small, preventing them from surpassing their own individualistic legacy. Does this sound like a boss you once had, a former president of the United States, a Floridian governor, or the CEO of an electric vehicle company who also tanked a once-popular social media platform?

Low-conscious leaders either use force to acquire power or they don't stand up for what most other people agree is best. Both are rooted in unintegrated trauma. From a Buddhist perspective, this is typically associated with *wounded* or *unhealed energy*. Synonymous with low-consciousness, unconscious leaders are often described as reactive—in that they "react from a 'story' about the past or an imagined future, and their personality, ego, or mind takes over. They are not free to lead from creative impulse, nor are they tuned in to what the moment is requiring of them."[1]

Looking at low-conscious leadership through the lens of neuroscience, "we now know that trauma compromises the brain area that communicates the physical, embodied feeling of being alive. These changes explain why traumatized individuals become hypervigilant to threat at the expense of spontaneously engaging in their day-to-day lives,"[2] says Bessel van der Kolk, MD, one of the foremost experts on the brain-body connection in healing. People who have not processed their trauma continue to repeat similar patterns time and again without gleaning insights from their experiences, and this explains why that is. It's easier to find compassion when you understand that they behave the way they do not because they want to, or because they are bad people, but because they are constantly in survival mode. Unconsciously, they are trying to keep their ego protected from a constant perception of threat.[3]

Maladaptive behavior is directly correlated to changes in the brain system.[4] Therefore, those with a people-controlling leadership style aren't inherently bad or broken; they're simply operating from a place of survival. They are on a quest for safety. The most ancient portion of our threat perception system, our reptilian brain, functions at speeds 80,000 times faster than our more modern, conscious, front-brain system counterpart. Gina Hayden, author of *Becoming a Conscious Leader*, explains that "within the deepest and oldest part of our brain lie the two small, almond-shaped amygdalae, whose job it is to scan the environment every five milliseconds for signs of friend or foe, risks and threats. Although our brain likes rewards, it is even more strongly wired to pick up threats—by five times as much, in fact."[5] Every five milliseconds.

The instinct for survival keeps our access to more expansive functions of the brain significantly impaired or entirely offline. If we're focused on the singular act of surviving, we have very little creativity or innovation available to us. We can only focus on the issue right in front of us, so our decisions can only be shortsighted and individualistic— forget about factoring others into the equation, whether they are current stakeholders or future generations.[6]

## How Did We Get Here?

As sociopolitical and economic landscapes have shifted in favor of more-better-faster-cheaper, leadership has become divisive. Think of some recent events. In March 2023, President Biden approved the largest proposed oil drilling project by a petroleum company on US federal land, within the National Petroleum Reserve-Alaska (NPR-A),[7] opting to save face with big oil—a decision based on survival and, quite literally, a need for approval. While Biden did take a positive step in the right direction in September 2023 when he canceled seven remaining oil and gas leases in the Arctic National Wildlife Refuge (ANWR)—and put protections in place for more than 13 million acres within the NPR-A[8]—about the same time, UK prime minister Rishi Sunak approved an oil and gas field north of Scotland that will have significant and environmentally costly effects for generations to come.[9] Then there is the governor of Florida, who in May 2023 signed into law a first-of-its-kind piece of legislation that prohibits public colleges nationwide from funding diversity, equity, and inclusion (DEI) programs—all in an effort to restrict race-related curriculum in higher education institutions.[10] Read: to protect white supremacy. Within 30 days, the governor of Texas followed suit. Delusion and disinformation to this extent, and hate to any extent, is failed leadership, regardless of political affiliation.

"Most leaders—whether in politics or business—fail," as organizational psychologist Dr. Tomas Chamorro-Premuzic puts bluntly. "That has always been the case: the majority of nations, companies, societies and organizations are poorly managed, as indicated by their longevity, revenues, and approval ratings, or by the effects they have on their citizens, employees, subordinates or members. Good leadership has always been the exception, not the norm."[11]

Why is that? Let's look at the evolution of leadership from how it was first defined through our present-day associations. In 2003, Miriam Grace presented at the International Leadership Association conference on the evolution of the word *leadership* in the English language over the last 1,000 years. She explained:

> The root word of leadership is *lead* from the Anglo-Saxon Old English word *loedan*, the causal form of *lithan*—to travel. The Oxford English Dictionary's (OED, 1989) first entry for the word *lead* is from 825 A.C.E. with a meaning defined as: "to cause to go along with oneself, to bring or take (a person or an animal) to a place." The OED indicates that a definition of lead that is closer

to the modern sense of leadership appears in the textual record around 1225 A.C.E. with the meaning: "to guide with reference to action and opinion; to bring by persuasion or counsel to or into a condition; to conduct by argument or representation to a conclusion; to induce to do something—said of persons, circumstances, evidence, etc." The use of the terms *persuasion* and *counsel* here are particularly interesting as these meanings were not attributed to the term leader until around 1828, when *Webster's An American Dictionary of the English Language* introduced the concepts of *influence* and *exercising of dominion* to define the concept of leadership.[12]

Essentially, we had it right out of the gate: to take others with us as we move forward. That evolved into guiding, influencing, counseling, conducting, and inspiring action in others—a harmonious balance of seemingly dualistic energies. We started to veer off course in the 1800s with the narrower definition of ruling, controlling, or having power over others. We were in the midst of the Industrial Revolution, during which time it was erroneously assumed that most employees could not think for themselves. Leaders thought they needed to be omniscient and direct daily tasks. They cared not at all about the health and safety of workers, nor the environment, but focused solely on productivity.[13]

After 1820 and into the mid- to late 1800s, several revolutionary movements fought for women's suffrage, limits on child labor, abolition, temperance, and prison reform. The economy was changing drastically, from one that was agricultural to one based on wages and the exchange of goods and services. What's interesting about the leadership of the three main 19th-century social reform movements—abolition, temperance, and women's rights—is that they were linked together and shared many of the same leaders. Its members advocated for holistic social change, in that leaders collaborated by sharing strategic thinking and new ideas with each other. The focus of reform just before the Civil War was abolitionism, and "leaders in both the temperance and women's rights movements consciously stepped aside while anti-slavery work took precedence."[14] They then returned to their agendas once the 13th Amendment was ratified.

Domination, control, and power were common leadership themes in the early 1900s, although it wasn't until the 1930s that the term *leader* was even applied in business.[15] Until the 1950s, America was nearly a wholly segregated society. The mindset of the day was solely production-focused, as post-WWII production demands drove leadership styles. Don Draper–style leaders dominated in business. They promoted their own achievements, directed others, were decisive, and committed themselves to their organizations, even if they felt isolated in the process.[16] That productivity-first mindset carried into the 21st century, as leadership was *autocratic* and *task-oriented*—not very different from what we've seen for the last 150 years. The focus was on hard skills and task completion.

Since the early 2000s, that has been changing at an accelerated pace. The conscious leadership movement in particular has been categorized as *collaborative* and *people-oriented*. It's about empowerment over power. There's nothing soft about soft skills; they are more valuable than ever, and tasks are being directed less and less from managers. Remote work has forced leaders to trust their people to do their jobs and meet organizational goals both autonomously and collaboratively with colleagues.

Most recently, we've witnessed and experienced dramatic shifts in the hallmarks of effective leadership, but many organizations are slow to adopt and adapt to the change, particularly if their leaders are resistant. Nearly 75 years ago, "if a leader had a heart, they had to pretend like they didn't; they had to hide it in order to succeed. In contrast to today, if leaders aren't heart-led, they have to pretend as though they are," says my dear friend and colleague Justin Foster.[17] We see this in the corporate arena just as much as we see it in nonprofit and governmental sectors. Change is not always welcomed—especially when systems and entire institutions have been designed and maintained to benefit a dominant group. Here, we're talking about cisgender, heterosexual, white men (and women).

The inflection point at which we find ourselves is best illustrated by the fact that we are in the midst of a sea change in what it means to be a leader, and many still cling to the familiarity of the only type of leadership we've known for 200 years. As soon as we embody a new reference point, we can begin to unravel the belief that a scarcity mindset protects the power we have and the power we might gain. Perhaps, it all comes down to having a finite mindset, which makes enemies of uncertainty and curiosity. If resistant leaders believe that by empowering others, there will be fewer resources for them, it makes sense that they would cling tightly to their power—erecting metaphoric citadels wherever they go. It makes sense that they rail against any change that threatens their status, wealth, or ego. All of this comes down to perceived threat (fear), which manifests as a scarcity mindset (the feeling of not having or being enough) and attachment to ego (the uncertainty of one's identity if something changes). However, the truth is that domination and love are simply incompatible, which is why heart-led leaders get further, faster by holding their people in high regard.

As you learn more about the correlation of trauma to leadership, it will become clearer that fear is always rooted in trauma; thoughts and behaviors are merely trailheads. But here's a question: It's not as if trauma appeared for the first time in the 1950s, so where was all the trauma? Trauma has actually been hiding in plain sight for a long time. And our production-focused, patriarchal leadership of the last two centuries is at the root of trauma's societal suppression—through the distraction of substances, sex, and overwork, among others. We can even try to compartmentalize the emotions that might surface, but eventually trauma seeps out—one way or another.

## My Turn to Be Bullied

When I was in eighth grade, I didn't know about trauma's influence on leadership characteristics. I had certainly never heard of generational trauma, nor did I have the tools to understand why wounded leaders abuse their subordinates. Unhealed trauma that is projected on those we lead can destroy one's sense of safety and self.

Being named Most Valuable Player of my volleyball team in middle school instilled confidence and a love for the sport. When tryouts were held freshman year of high school, I was one of the top picks for the junior varsity volleyball team. As a sophomore I made varsity, and by junior year I had been named to the All-County team as a setter. Several college scouts had their eyes on me.

I accelerated to the level I did because I had played competitive club volleyball in the off-season, attending some of the top summer programs at the University of Massachusetts at Amherst and University of North Carolina at Chapel Hill to work intensively on my setting, serving, and defensive skills. Instead of choosing the club team run by my volleyball coach—an entitled white man who had coached my father when he was in high school—I chose to play for the team coached by one of our high school's competitors. She was driven, approachable, well-respected, and a highly conscious leader. I knew that the training would be harder and require more of my time, the level of competition would be higher, and it was more expensive, but my chances of getting a full ride to college were also much greater. And it felt important to prove my worth in that way—that I could essentially pay for my own education.

I witnessed my varsity coach berate many teammates publicly and privately over the course of those years. He shamed some girls about their body weight, others about their performance. It was never constructive. It was always abusive, almost masochistic. I knew his demeanor, language, and approach was wrong, but I was never courageous enough to stand up to him, to say something on their behalf.

Until it was my turn to be bullied. What I had not factored into my decision to play for the more competitive off-season club were the repercussions I encountered when I returned senior year to play for my high school—coached by a man who needed to punish, not praise, me. Though my intention was purely to challenge myself and pay for my education with an athletic scholarship, his ego was bruised. There was no way he was going to let a young girl embarrass him or circumvent the club team he led. So he took it upon himself to make my senior season a living hell. He despised the coach of my club team. Because some of his own players chose her team over his in the off-season, he wouldn't even shake her hand after matches when our high school or club teams competed against one another.

Even though I was named the best setter in the county and in the top three in the entire state of New York the prior year, I didn't start a single match my senior year. When I did get playing time, it was typically as a defensive specialist—not as a setter, the position for which I would be recruited by colleges. And I was only allowed to step foot on the court when our team was playing a tough competitor, when the chance of a loss on *his* record was simply not an option.

During practice after school each day, I was relegated to running laps and collecting balls while everyone else honed their skills. I spent time setting against the walls of our gymnasium when he wasn't looking or stepped out. At a certain point, his verbal abuse and bullying tactics became so traumatizing that a lawyer advised my family to ensure that I had someone else with me at all times whenever he spoke to me. It became unsafe for me to be alone with him. The athletic director got involved as well because I was deemed *insubordinate* by my coach—for advocating for my own sense of safety and for following the attorney's directive. No action was ever taken against him except that a formal complaint was filed away in the athletic director's office. I later learned that it was added to a stack of reports filed over the years due to similar mistreatment of young girls and his abuse of patriarchal power.

As an intimidation tactic, he physically blocked me from leaving the back seat of a school bus once after an away match. In some way, I was also waiting for the day that he tried to grab or shove me out of sheer anger and frustration. I had been preparing for it. I would run through the scenario in my mind. It always ended with me screaming in his face, "Get off of me! No one lays a hand on me!" I felt the volcano of emotional eruption inside just thinking about it. It was the projection of what the younger version of me wanted to say to my mother every time she grabbed, slapped, scratched, pushed, pulled, or hit me. With my coach though, the stakes were much lower because I wasn't looking to earn his love. Even so, my guts were a frenetic ball of energy, while I gritted my teeth and tried to act like his hateful words and bullying had no effect on me. I just wanted it to end.

The team made it to the state finals that year. But while defense was what we lacked most, I was rotated into the backcourt during the championship match. He probably hated that I was such a good player, but he wanted to win by any means necessary. I decided earlier on in the season that if my punishment was to be invisible to college scouts as a setter, then I was going to be the best defensive specialist I could be. I had my club coach to thank for that level of training, inspiration, and encouragement as I became an even more well-rounded player.

We won the New York State Women's Volleyball Championship that year. It was a career-high feat for our coach. And even in the backcourt, I didn't go unnoticed for the role I played. Yet every college recruiter who spoke to my coach seemed perplexed about why I hadn't been setting—and why, in conversations with him, he was making me out to be an "insubordinate player." After all, I had been named All-County setter the year prior, and the way in which I interacted with my teammates was certainly not in alignment with his portrayal of me. Not to mention the straight As on my academic record. He went out of his way to make sure I stayed small.

As I was researching and writing this book, I discovered an additional negative impact from that entire experience. In a 2004 study, adolescent children of mentally ill mothers reported high levels of attachment to their schools because they fill an important void of order and stability in the lives of traumatized children[18]—and so we respond positively to school settings.

For many trauma survivors, school and after-school activities like sports are the healthiest parts of our lives. School was a place where life made sense to me, for the most part. Since that was where routine existed, where the roles of adults and students had clear delineation, and adults meant what they said, what he stole from me during a pivotal period was *safety*. I wasn't safe at home, and now I wasn't safe at school either. Have you ever felt that hiding from the world, retreating into your own corner, was the only way to ensure survival—whether physically, mentally, emotionally, or spiritually?

## Hurt People Hurt People

Years later, I heard that my former volleyball coach had passed away. At first, I felt a wash of relief. He could no longer treat young athletes the way he did; I certainly wasn't the first, nor was I the last. More than that, though, I felt a strange sense of gratitude. He showed me what toxic, fear-based leadership looked like, sounded like, and felt like to those simply seeking guidance. Another catalyst on my journey, he provided the opportunity for me to stand in the face of imposed adversity—even if I was literally trembling or in tears most of the time. He embodied the antiquated, misogynistic paradigm, where ineffective, so-called leaders bully, take credit for themselves, and step on those below them for illusory survival—to keep anyone from rising above their own spotlight.

As van der Kolk reminds us, "Angry people live in angry bodies."[19] Unconscious leaders often take credit for the accomplishments of others, display a lack of compassion, see vulnerability as weakness, can be walled up, are always on guard or defensive, consistently exhibit emotionally reactive behaviors, and are attached to the egoic need to be right in most every circumstance.

Although I certainly didn't feel it at the time during high school, I was railing against this form of so-called leadership. I displayed vulnerability, and I kept showing up day after day despite his intention, perhaps even personal mission, to break me. What he saw as emotional weakness would become one of my greatest strengths. He had clearly underestimated me. He had no idea how I'd been training my entire young life under my mother's abuse not only to stand in the face of provocation but to emerge even stronger. He didn't know that I already had something to prove well before him.

I also recognize now how he served as a mirror to my own lack of self-love and need for control. Years later, through Buddhist psychology study, I have learned to have compassion for the conditions in his own life that caused him to remain this version of himself until the day he died.

Instead of making me shrink, the entire experience inadvertently prepared me well for what I would face working in male-dominant industries—and with dominant males, for that matter. While I know that I would never treat people the way he did, I am grateful to have experienced the opposite of *stewardship*. He showed me the shadow side of leadership. In retrospect, he also taught me the importance of justice and the strength of my own voice. I'm proud of the courage I found deep inside to be able to stand in the face of it all.

You've heard the phrase "hurt people hurt people." Wounds become scars, and physical scarring is a metaphor for unconscious or low-conscious leadership. Scars become rigid, inflexible, and hard. Healthy growth ceases. And a higher level of reactivity is probable when prodded. Gaining a better understanding of childhood trauma's impact on one's leadership style allows us to shift from judgment and blame to understanding and compassion.

## How Do We Deal with Low-Conscious Leaders?

On the one hand, we need to protect ourselves from the projections of low-conscious leaders' past trauma. On the other hand, there are times when we feel that we have no choice but to engage with a boss, authority figure, family member, or community leader. Most people cannot immediately find a new job or relocate. So how do we operate in the world with *leaders who live in angry bodies?*

Whether we are forced to engage with those who operate completely unaware of their impact on anyone or anything else, or we see some low-conscious characteristics within ourselves, remember that we have agency. Yes, it's exhausting. In the moments when we feel like things might never get better, rest is also necessary. Zooming out can be helpful to realize how much space and energy these interactions consume in our life. From there, we can decide if we'd like to change that and what we will commit to doing to make that happen. Setting strong and healthy boundaries—verbally, physically, and energetically—is an effective way to teach low-conscious leaders what you will not accept.

Know that all of these experiences are part of healing your own wounds, and that you're about to learn a whole new way of being, both to deal with low-consciousness outside of yourself as well as to integrate your own trauma into your leadership style.

# 3

---

# The Wound in the Room

DURING A SEMINAR in January 2022 entitled "Mental Illness or Adaptation?" I had the opportunity to ask Dr. Maté how unhealed childhood trauma impacts organizational leaders. He responded with a quote by Robert Hare: "Not all psychopaths are in prison, some are in the boardroom." He continued:

> When you actually look at the study of business executives and politicians, you find a lot of sociopathic characteristics—more than the rest of the population—because they can succeed in this crazy culture. A lot of these people are very driven, traumatized individuals who have to be in control, who have to demean others. They have to have more power all the time to enhance their undernourished sense of self. And our society rewards these people. We call them prime ministers and presidents and business executives. It's the nature of our toxic culture that will keep this going. Look at something like climate change. I don't think anyone still disputes that climate change is happening, but there are people who are still pursuing profits and directly contributing to [climate change]. Yet, since they're behaving this way by way of legitimate businesses, they can [indirectly] kill millions and be called brilliant free marketeers. So that's the nature of the society that we live in. And this is what's called normal.[1]

While calling some low-conscious business leaders *psychopaths* might seem provocative, the characteristics of both of these personality disorders is rooted in a lack of empathy—an inability to establish meaningful relationships, and a constant attempt to control others through threats, manipulation, or aggression. About a decade ago, some research suggested that one in five chief executives could be considered a *corporate psychopath*, but further insight into those studies revealed that psychopathy wasn't found just at the highest levels of leadership, nor was it exclusive to corporations; psychopathy was present at director, managerial, and staff levels alike—and was found in nonprofits, government organizations, and small businesses. I have chosen phrases like *low-conscious leaders*, *wounded leaders*, and *people-controlling leaders* instead of *corporate psychopathy* or *corporate bullying* for this reason.

Intrinsically, People Controllers who exhibit low-conscious leadership characteristics are stuck in a defensive mindset. They view resources as finite, believing them to be scarce even when they are abundant. They feel they must win at all costs, and that everyone else must lose, whether that is a conscious, subconscious, or unconscious desire. Stepping on others elevates their own ego and keeps them from facing themselves.

The extrinsic motivations to remain in this state are the societal rewards that perpetuate the maladaptive behavior to which Dr. Maté refers. Low-conscious leaders might also see their primary objective as achieving success, no matter the toll it takes on the people within the organization. On more subtle levels, unconscious leaders are partly unaware of how their everyday behaviors impact others. Even People Pleasers can feel as though they need to have all of the answers or take tasks on themselves, without realizing how that both disempowers and distances those whom they lead. They don't see how it signals to people that their leader doesn't value their input or trust their problem-solving abilities.

Unsurprisingly, the organizational systems we have in place are designed to incentivize both people-controlling and people-pleasing aspects of low-conscious leadership. Those who climb the corporate ladder to senior-most positions typically do so based on financial metrics—rarely, if ever, based on how well they support and collaborate with their colleagues.

## Inner Wisdom Requires Willingness

Trauma is at the root of the maladaptive behaviors that leaders exhibit, so healing cannot be unimportant. Yet I don't think it's merely a blind spot for the vast majority either. I believe most people have an inner knowing that there is something in their past that they'd prefer not to face, admit, or work through. I believe it comes down to *willingness*.

The connection between trauma and effective leadership has not yet become a mainstream conversation because very few people are willing to talk about the invisible wound in the room. As my friend and DEI consultant K. Michael Slater says, "Everyone's got trauma, but no one's comparing notes."[2] Yet if we knew about or could see one another's history, we would treat each other very differently. This is the basis of compassion—one of the four fundamentals of high-conscious leadership.

## Pain Avoidance and Pain Bias

We don't talk about trauma because we don't understand ourselves, let alone other people. When we were younger, no one taught us how to process emotions like fear, sadness, grief, or anger. We learned that talking about our darker feelings, or even having them, was unwelcome. We weren't allowed to get mad. When we cried, our tears were quelled. We came to interpret our emotions as bad and even a burden on our caregivers. Our role was to ensure ease for them so our needs might be met. Or it became clear that we needed to stay hidden in order to survive in the places where we grew up. A smaller percentage experienced neither of these, but were not exactly given the space to talk through and integrate what we were feeling. This is the root of pain avoidance in adulthood.

What's worse is that many of us were also on the receiving end of pain bias, in that our caregivers—out of their own discomfort with emotion and unprocessed trauma—told us that we were fine and were not really experiencing anything difficult, essentially the *get over it* style of caretaking that many continue to perpetuate because they don't yet understand the impact of invalidating children's experiences. This is how physical, mental, and emotional wounds get overlooked and can deeply impact one's sense of worth.

It doesn't stop there though. As we get older, we see in our sick care system the clearest examples of physical pain bias. Conventional doctors, dentists, orthopedists, and other medical professionals can be biased, in that they don't always believe patients' experiences. Those whose pain is most typically undermined by clinicians—women and people of color—might also be less skeptical of the pain reports of others.[3] Thus, the cycle of pain bias is real, and it's another related reason why so few people feel comfortable and safe to talk about their suffering. According to Brandon Boring and colleagues, "This belief is consequential in clinical settings, where pain reported by patients is often dismissed, diminished, or invalidated—sometimes embedded within unsubstantiated narratives of attention-seeking, drug-seeking, or malingering. Such prevalent beliefs often go unchecked, allowing entry for bias into pain assessment and contribute to suboptimal care and continued suffering."[4] It is not a sign of weakness, nor a genetic deficit to experience posttraumatic effects.

## The Distance Between One Another Is Ourselves

Since this is the inflection point at which we find ourselves—unwell but unwilling to dive headfirst into healing—where do we go from here? What will it take for us to start believing each other? How do we normalize bringing psychological wounds into the light to be normalized once and for all?

Before trauma can be integrated on a collective level, we must change more than our mindset; we must unlearn the messaging from our youngest years and give the adult version of us permission to feel, emote, process, and rewire what's been deeply programmed. What I'm calling for goes well beyond the box-checking that happens during Mental Health Awareness Month in May in the United States. I'm talking about championing vulnerability in our leaders, destigmatization in our workplaces, and trusting ourselves above all else.

## Vulnerability

As I explained in the Introduction, tremendous vulnerability is required of leaders when sharing parts of themselves with others. Since vulnerability has historically been viewed as weakness, internally that becomes a self-perpetuating agreement. Continuing to subscribe to the old paradigm—the avoidance of being seen as vulnerable in any way—only creates a wider chasm between a leader and those they lead.

If self-aware leaders wish to influence the culture of their organizations and lead by example, vulnerability is the way. Leaders who are open about their own adversities and their need for support in decision-making or implementation are seen as human. Higher levels of dedication and respect naturally follow.

Yet there's a prerequisite to vulnerability that no one really talks about, and that is the ability to be vulnerable with and within yourself. Being honest is about feeling all of our feelings and the experiences we're having in order to be fully present. Doing that without numbing, minimizing. or outright avoiding is especially difficult if we've never engaged with ourselves in that way. Yet it's the first step in being able to share parts of ourselves with one or a few trusted people as a way to build enough muscle and evidence that we can share with those in our larger social group, organization, community, or the public at large.

## Destigmatization

Mental health has been stigmatized in society and workplaces for centuries. Just as employees have demanded that leadership do better when it comes to DEI, we need to rally around destigmatizing mental health challenges.

Mental health conditions do not correlate with performance, which means that when executives and other leaders who perform at high levels talk openly about their challenges, the stigma begins to dissipate more quickly.[5]

We must start within our own interior because we must first overcome the internalized stigma we might have about our own experiences.

From an extrinsic perspective, we fear being judged for being abnormal or unstable. We're afraid of being seen as incompetent, unreliable, or unprofessional. If we don't start with breaking down what we have absorbed from society about mental health and keep our experiences to ourselves, the stigma will live on.

## Inner Work

There's deep, ongoing work to be done, and most of us prefer distraction. The enemy is not trauma itself; it's the inadequate systems and modalities—rooted in the Western, pathological view of trauma—that cause us to remain in a repetitive mode that seeks repair outside of ourselves. While many of these can be tools to help us cope with our pain, bringing a problem-solving mindset to trauma integration actually makes it worse.

Psychiatric diagnoses can be examples of this. The label of a diagnosis becomes, for many, a part of how they identify in the world and are identified by others. Often, a diagnosis is made by a doctor or two— humans who can be wrong, and therefore inform the wrong treatment, or apply a Band-Aid medication. If symptoms are not understood as the manifestation of trauma, and Western medicine doesn't account for how people have developed creative survival strategies that no longer serve them, then the reparative loop simply continues, to the detriment of the person already suffering.

Trauma is not a problem to be fixed; it's a part of us that must be met, seen from different perspectives, reprogrammed, and used as a means to reparent the younger version of ourselves whose basic psychological needs went unmet. We grow up and assume positions of leadership, also assuming that we will somehow magically outgrow the coping strategies we implored to survive.

On the contrary, those strategies only calcify. The grooves in our psyche become ruts, and we call them our *comfort zone*. To remain in that zone, keeping the ego safe from threat to itself, we develop behavioral dependencies and substance addictions. When we view leaders through this lens, these are all markers for inner work so that we might integrate past trauma.

## Survivor Leaders

In my research, I came across a dissertation from over a decade ago in which a doctoral candidate explored trauma's impact on leadership in educational leaders. It took me some time to track down Dr. Wendy Lynn Mills, but she graciously agreed to an interview about her work, entitled "Survivor Leaders: A Grounded Theory Inquiry into Leadership Practices of Childhood Trauma Survivors."[6]

Dr. Mills set out to explore how the experience of trauma in childhood influenced the professional practice of leaders—of educational institutions, in this case. None of her research participants, incest and sexual-based trauma survivors, had ever spoken about their experiences until being interviewed for the study. It was the opportunity to share their stories for the benefit of helping others that made them willing to do so. When asked what they would change about their past, the overwhelming response was *the mitigation of others' pain*, such as that experienced by siblings.[7]

What Dr. Mills found was that survivor leaders had a greater emphasis on collaboration with and feedback from stakeholders versus those who did not experience sexual abuse during childhood. They placed much greater emphasis on checking in, creating shared agreements and mutual understanding with those they lead. Having had the experience of being overlooked and making themselves invisible to avoid setting off the abuse, they had more of a distributed, transformational leadership style.[8]

Survivor leaders cared about the support staff in their schools more than others, particularly disadvantaged and marginalized populations, because they didn't want them to experience the same invisibility that they had to rely on for survival.[9] The paradox is fascinating, and this is an example of how the trauma experienced by leaders can naturally lend itself to more conscious leadership behaviors.

Another finding from the research was that survivor leaders subconsciously led in a way that their organizations could be sustained without them.[10] "Part of that," says Dr. Mills, "is that severe trauma at a young age tends to make us not think about longevity for ourselves. This manifests into doing and giving all we can in the present, which is what's really underneath the addiction of workaholism."[11] In toxic (and even some nontoxic) workplaces, overworking is not only seen as acceptable, it is celebrated. Long hours and poor boundaries are often called dedication. These behaviors are rewarded with praise and promotion. For survivor leaders, it's even more difficult to break free from environments in which our coping strategies from childhood continue to be rewarded. That feedback loop keeps us stuck in positions of familiarity, even though there seems to be some discomfort in knowing that there is a different way for us to live and lead.

All leaders have experienced some degree of trauma in their lives that influences their personality, behavior, and leadership style. And the ways in which trauma manifests *sets us up to be* conscious leaders; the difference in whether or not we awaken to that consciousness is in whether or not we choose to do the inner work.

# 4

## Why Now?

BETWEEN A DEEPLY introspective period when we all came face to face with the reality of our lives, an anti-oppression movement spurred by the murder of George Floyd, basic human rights being stripped away from us on both national and state levels in the United States, genocide in the Middle East, and climate change flooding our front doors or burning them down, it's no wonder why so many of us have been brought to the breaking point.

Organizational leaders are inundated with the (rightful) demands of employees and customers, sociopolitical concerns, environmental responsibility, and profitability—whether there are shareholders to answer to or not. And many are without an understanding of how they became who they are in their leadership role, or what's needed to influence change more effectively.

Operating within antiquated systems are the command-and-control leaders who could have changed the trajectory of our world—but made decisions not to do so. They are now starting to feel the force of revolution amid a major paradigm shift. Some leaders have started to wake up and realize that there has to be a better, more viable way forward. But let's be clear: we have a very long way to go before we can associate *stewardship* with leadership. Stewardship is in the careful tending of something that has been entrusted to us. It's the responsibility to maintain, protect, and nourish all beings under our care. While this is not at all how we currently think of leadership, we can and will get there.

## An Increasing Interest in New Leadership Philosophies

Many people are familiar with *servant leadership*, in which the goal of the person at the helm is to serve by putting their people's needs first. *Transformational leadership* is a theory whereby a leader works with teams or groups beyond their immediate self-interests, identifies needed change, creates a vision to guide that change, and then executes the change in tandem with committed members of a group. Since about 2014, there's been a swirl of interest in the practice of *conscious leadership*, which was born from conscious capitalism—a movement coined by the now retired co founder and CEO of Whole Foods John Mackey and marketing professor and author Rajendra (Raj) Sisodia.

Today, conscious leadership has become more than a catchphrase. It simply makes good business sense because it demonstrates impact beyond profit, which creates a sustainability loop. I would go so far as to say that conscious leadership has become non-negotiable for the majority of employees and consumers, but unfortunately not most of our leaders. We continue to see how some resist the notion that they need to evolve beyond the ego, invite others to the table, and ensure ecological regeneration.

Research commissioned in 2018 by Healthy Companies International, labeled the *Conscious Index*, found that "82% of Americans feel there would be less turmoil in the world if leaders were more conscious. 89% believe that conscious leaders drive significant organizational improvements, including 87% believing that conscious leadership leads to better financial performance. But we have a serious perception gap: 94% of C-suite executives believe they are very or somewhat conscious while only half of working adults observe highly conscious behavior in their leaders."[1] What do we do with a disparity of this magnitude?

## Conscious Leadership Mandates

On August 6, 2021, the SEC approved Nasdaq's plans to require listed companies to meet specific race and gender targets in pursuit of DEI improvement.[2] Their charge to public corporations was to have at least one female board director and another board member who identifies as either a racial minority or a member of the LGBTQIA+ community. Additionally, they would have to release statistics about their board composition. This doesn't seem like much of a requirement, but as of 2020, more than 75% of listed companies did not meet these requirements. Shocked by that stat? Neither was I.

Yet the findings are obvious. Companies in the top quartile of executive teams that are gender-diverse are 25% more likely to have above average profitability.[3] Ethnic diversity for executive teams means they are 36% more likely to outperform their less or non-diverse peer corporations. If the resistance is not monetarily based, then what is it that has historically made homogeneous boards of cisgender, heterosexual white men exclude women, people of color, and those who identify as LGBTQIA+?

Some chalk it up to our *patriarchal society*, where a male-dominated power structure pervades personal relationships, organizations, institutions, and systems,[4] where attributes associated with feminine energy are undervalued, while attributes regarded as energetically masculine are privileged. Others call it part of *systemic oppression*—the intentional disadvantaging of groups of people based on their identity while advantaging members of the dominant group.

Personally, I believe that oppressive leadership is one of the most severe forms of low-consciousness. As author, comedian, and activist Alok Vaid-Menon asks, "Are you fighting for freedom or are you fighting for privilege? Because privilege is the ability to monopolize. Privilege is the ability to do what was done to you to other people. The way that we heal pain is not by transmitting it, it's by transforming it. So, your pain is valid. But your use of that pain, your weaponization of that pain to harm other people, is not valid. Let's interrupt the cycle of trauma."[5]

The fact that diversity and inclusion targets need to be mandated demonstrates how aggressively white, male executives force their own supremacist agendas. So afraid of losing what's long been in their grasp, they find it difficult to fathom the idea that power and wealth distribution among their leadership teams would benefit their corporations. The sad truth, though, is that diversity and inclusion mandates are ineffective if they are merely box-checking mechanisms. "To fully benefit from increased racial and gender diversity, organizations must adopt a learning orientation and be willing to change the corporate culture and power structure. . . . To dismantle systems of discrimination and subordination, leaders must undergo the same shifts of heart, mind, and behavior that they want for the organization as a whole and then translate those personal shifts into real, lasting change in their companies."[6]

Contrary to agendas of privilege, conscious leaders are aware of their own egos. They understand the difference between power and force, and why both are necessary. From a Buddhist perspective, power is wisdom while force is action. The wisdom of conscious leaders is that they "actively seek to put in place structure, processes and activities that enable many voices to be heard and for collective intelligence to be harvested."[7] They also understand that overharvesting and depleting other provisions doesn't set future generations up for success.

## Environmental Care Commitments

Cultural, *ecological,* and economic. We can't talk about conscious leadership without the second aspect of the triple-bottom-line success measurement. In the naturalized view, land care is actually more important than people and profit because you cannot have the latter without the former intact, though the practice of conscious leadership holds all three on equal plane. As our global temperature rises due to human-inflicted climate change, we will all be forced to adapt to a new reality year after year. We're already encountering more frequent heat waves and wildfires, higher sea levels, water quality and supply issues, the increased spread of diseases, and loss of human, plant, and animal life.[8]

We have passed the midway mark of "The 2030 Agenda for Sustainable Development," where world leaders of all UN Member States committed to the 17 Sustainable Development Goals (SDGs). Written in 2015, the SDGs served to *stimulate action* on behalf of people, planet, prosperity, peace, and partnership.[9] In many ways, it was and is a universal plan for conscious leadership.

The reduction of greenhouse gas emissions—down to zero—requires collective effort. It is the responsibility of businesses, institutions, and citizens of every nation to ensure habitability for future generations. Gen Z is making this their priority. On August 14, 2023, in a landmark climate change trial, a Montana judge ruled in favor of young activists who argued that the state's fossil fuel emissions add to the climate emergency, have unlawfully caused them harm, and are unconstitutional.[10] So when political and corporate leaders either discount the validity of climate change or make decisions about energy projects that fly in the face of the climate crisis, it sends the message that the issue is not that serious. Trust environmental scientists. Trust what Mother Earth is telling us.

We won't for long, but right now we have a choice. We can either choose to continue resisting the collective shift toward a more equitable world, or we can do the right thing right now. We can choose to do the brave, hard work of taking responsibility for healing ourselves and our relationship with nature so we can lead our people and organizations into a finer future.

To create higher consciousness in the world, we must *heal to lead.*

# PART

# II

# Preparing for the Journey

*"When we don't pay attention to the shadow dimensions of ourselves, they sabotage our leadership."*[1]

—Barrett C. Brown
*EXECUTIVE COACH, ADVISOR, AND SPEAKER*

ADDRESSING OUR OWN dysfunctional behavior is difficult. It's the thing we avoid because we fear what others might find out about us, oscillating between the conscious and the subconscious. Much greater than that fear, though, is what we might find out about ourselves that's unconscious.

Beyond what holds us back internally from addressing our core wounds is the society in which we live, constantly messaging that there are certain things we just don't talk about. However, our responsibility, especially in positions of power, is to bring it all into the light.

Unfortunately, we all still carry some amount of social conditioning that trauma is irrelevant, taboo, and certainly has no place in professional settings—that it's not a problem in leadership. And, that's right. Trauma is not *a problem* among leaders. Trauma is *the problem* among leaders.

The movement of high-conscious leadership is urgently needed, as our local school boards, state governments, national corporations and infrastructures, global economies, and ecological systems are all converging at the same corner point. But where are we owning how we can do better? When will we start to understand how our upbringing and formative experiences are negatively influencing our behavior as leaders and the decisions we make? Everyone who is impacted by our choices is suffering in some way if we have not worked to integrate our trauma, and the consequences are already inside of our homes, within our workplaces, threatening our democracy, and destroying the land and her more-than-human inhabitants.

From a place of active healing and integration, we have the power to do things differently. If it doesn't feel important enough to do for yourself, consider this: through our own inner development, we help others come home to themselves and contribute more fully in the world. Our vulnerability gives them the permission and safety to pursue a healthier existence.

I'm going to share an incredibly personal and raw story with you. It's one of many poignant moments that influenced who I became as a leader, and it's rooted in the physical abuse I experienced inside my home, with my mother. **If this is a sensitive topic for you, the following story (and others throughout the book) might be activating or leave you feeling tender. Please care for yourself in the ways that work best for you.**

# 5

## Contextualizing Trauma

As MUCH AS I was unknowingly becoming a natural leader in many areas of my life, I all but disappeared on too little love and a lack of self-worth. It required me to contort myself into an impossibly perfect persona from a young age. My mother looked at me with the contempt she had for herself—and as "the other woman" in my father's life, as if there was a finite amount of his love to go around and I was getting too much. But how could a child rationalize any of that?

If I could be less emotional and become adept at my endeavors— academically, athletically, creatively—then perhaps I would be worthy of her acceptance, affection, and adoration. If I starved my body or purged the food I ate, I might be thin enough to gain her approval. If I didn't tell anyone how verbally and emotionally abusive she was, her disparaging language would be protected behind closed doors. And if I never fought back when she took her rage out on my small body, it would all be over sooner. The mindfuck was that the more I tried to be perfect, the more she competed with and hurt me.

### The Night I Killed My Mother

At 16 years old, a junior in high school, my body was strong and I had gained confidence through honor roll, athletic leadership, and in a romantic relationship. After softball practice one night, I walked in the front door of my house. My brother was watching TV in the living room, my mother midstride from the kitchen. Whatever snarky, cutting comment she made as I entered, I countered with something equal in weight. I struck a nerve because she flew into an instant rage. She leapt toward me, but the door was already closed behind me. I was pinned. Holding a half-eaten apple in my left hand, I was able to hold her back with my raised, right forearm. Her sharp fingernails embedded into my skin as she gripped my arm, a second-best as she was trying to get at my face and hair. At that moment, I didn't feel the familiar piercing of those talons, I was solely focused on the realization that I was stronger than my mother. Much stronger.

In the midst of her advance, though, I dropped the apple and immediately bent over to pick it up. As I was fumbling, she bent down, picked up one of the high heels she had worn to work that day, raised it in the air, and planted the stem of it in the back of my skull. I felt the warm gush of blood and burst into tears. I swung the front door open and ran up the street to where my father was visiting my uncle, five houses from ours. When I arrived at the bottom of the steps where the two of them were talking outside, my dad took one look at me and said, "What did she do this time?"

He wasn't living with us at the time, but he went to talk to her. Classically, she denied the event, said I slipped and cracked my head on the floor and I was just overreacting again. But I was 16. I knew exactly what had happened; I no longer second-guessed whose version of the story was accurate like I did when I was five or seven or nine. I felt anger in my body, again, and quickly pushed it downward. I would swallow every ounce of rage to ensure I was nothing like her.

That night I had a dream. I was in a heated altercation with my mother, except this time I didn't just let her scream in my face. I didn't hold her at bay with one arm. I didn't run to my room and lock the door to escape. I fought back for the very first time. She was in a familiar fury, teeth bared and ripping my skin. With an ominous calm, I wrapped my hands around her throat and held her up against a wall, near that same entryway. As she kept fighting, I kept squeezing. My thumbs pressed into her trachea, harder and with more pressure. Her eyes shone in fear for the first time in my life, but I didn't waver.

I felt unaffected by the emotion on her face. Finally, she attempted to take one last small breath and then I felt her body go limp, expiring between my bare hands as she slid down the wall onto the floor. I had strangled and killed my mother.

I felt a sense of relief wash over my body and immediately began to cry—not because of what I had just done, but for the version of me as a little kid that no longer had to live in fear. I woke up from that dream in the middle of the night, terrified at the visual and also at the level of built-up anger housed in my body. I knew what I had to do. For someone with perfect attendance since the fifth grade, my plan was both serious and necessary. I waited until she left for work and packed up everything from my room that could fit in my 1974 Pontiac LeMans, called my boyfriend, and drove to his family's house to stay there for a while.

There was no way I could safely live in my home any longer. Either she was going to kill me, or I was going to off her like I did in my dream. And I didn't want to spend the rest of my life in jail. Guarding us from one another, I took the lead from afar by playing the protector, establishing boundaries for myself. It was an anxiety-filled decision because she was so unpredictable. *What if she comes home from work early, before I've been able to pack everything? What if the school calls her at work to ask why I didn't show up today? What if she drives over to my boyfriend's house and demands that I come home?* Even though I was stronger, physical strength couldn't make 16 years of terror disappear, and certainly not in less than 24 hours.

I made it out of the house and to my boyfriend's safely. The school never called. I don't remember if I phoned home that night, left a note in my bedroom, or did nothing at all. The details beyond driving away became a nonessential blur in the bank of my memories. What I do recall vividly, however, is that seven years later, when she and I were trying to repair our relationship—hashing things out over a bottle of wine—she was focused on making sure that I was made to feel guilty for what it was like for *her* to arrive home from work that day. "Why can't you see how that made me feel, Kelly, coming home to see your bedroom completely empty? Do you know how hurt I was?" I never told her about the dream. I was wise enough by then to know that it would absolutely be used against me.

Choosing to leave put me in a vulnerable spot, and it was also a turning point for me. As a young leader-in-the-making, it was one of many opportunities I would be given to assert boundaries against being bullied by wounded figures in my life. It became more obvious over time that there was no way I could heal while remaining in the same toxic environment. Call it survival or intuition, I knew that leaving was my only option to live; there was no question mark. Looking back, it was also the first time I chose myself. It was the first moment when I stood up, protected little Kelly, and said, "never again."

I would love to tell you that I never gave her the chance to hurt me again, but my desire to be loved by my mother was so strong that it was difficult to avoid stepping into the line of fire for the chance of even a drop of adoration from her. Against my better judgment, I shared with her the very personal, very vulnerable story about the night I contemplated ending my life. I thought that if I exposed a little more of myself, perhaps she would have no choice but to see me, finally feel something for me, and console me in my pain. She did shed a single tear when I told her, but on another night when we were trying to talk things out, she got defensive over something I said. Things were getting heated and I knew it might soon be time to leave her house. Before I could recalibrate the conversation, she reached into her mental vault of weaponry and pulled out the dagger that almost killed me on the spot. "Remember when you told me about the time you thought about killing yourself?. . . I wish you had done it!"

What I wish I had done was to keep that experience to myself, sharing it only with those I could trust, those who would keep that safe and hold it as sacred. In my attempt to gain my mother's love with one last pull at her heartstrings, I forgot how vengeful her own wounds made her. I was inconsolable.

By the time I was 24, now a full year into business ownership, I suggested for a fifth time that we go to see a therapist together to talk about our relationship, We would either do that, or there would be no relationship whatsoever. It was the ultimatum a child never wants to give their mother, but also knows that if they don't, they'll find themself gasping for air in a toxic brew for the rest of their life. To my surprise, she agreed to go. I set up an appointment with a therapist in her town whom I'd never seen before. I scheduled it in the early evening so it didn't interfere with her workday, and I agreed to pay for the sessions in full. I thought I'd closed every loophole. As the date drew nearer, my intuition said she'd bail, but I was cautiously optimistic. Thankfully, I wasn't driving when I dialed her number. "I'm not going to be able to make it to the appointment on Tuesday," she said.

"You're not going to be able to make it on Tuesday, or you're not going to make it ever? Before you answer that, I want to remind you of what I said initially; this is the only way forward for us." With that, she said, "I can't make it, ever." My heart dropped into the pit of my stomach and I went numb. "You understand that you're choosing not to have a relationship with me, not to be in my life at all?" Maybe she thought I was bluffing. Maybe she felt so cornered that she had to take back control in the situation and simultaneously hurt me one last time. But I had left one piece unconsidered—the one where my mother's fear about facing herself, or her fear of being exposed, was so strong that she would give up a relationship with one of her children.

That was the last time I spoke to my mother. I haven't had contact with her for nearly two decades. That final discarding was the only way to feel some modicum of control on her part—and maybe on mine as well. The constant rejection and abuse is what ultimately led me to enact the boundary where we would either collaborate and do the work together or part ways. When she opted for the latter, I had come to the conclusion that if I wanted any chance at living a healthy life, I needed to stay the course and disconnect from her completely. It was the most intense form of boundary-setting I've enacted to date. Now I can see that I saved my own life.

In retrospect, I also subconsciously developed the need to protect my psyche, my ego, and my heart from the ripping emotions of rejection and abandonment. This is known as a *Mother Wound*—"an attachment trauma that creates a sense of confusion and devastation in a child's psyche. It instills deeply rooted beliefs that make the child feel unloved, abandoned, unworthy of care, and even fearful of expressing themselves."[1] If this resonates, there is more on this in Chapter 11. From a spiritual perspective, there is a "feeling of being disconnected and alienated from a higher power and life itself," according to Bethany Webster, author of *Discovering the Inner Mother*.[2]

That maternal trauma set the tone for the next 15 years of my life—and I became masterful at the art of disguising it all, especially as a leader. I'll get into what that looked like in personal and business relationships in subsequent chapters, but I think it's important to pause here and reflect on your own life for a moment.

Are there painful events, conversations, or experiences that stand out in your mind from your early years?

What did you make them mean about you back then—and do you still harbor some of those false narratives?

## Knowing Ourselves

Understanding others is core to being able to lead effectively. Yet how can we come to understand others if we never come to know ourselves first?

My own desire to belong certainly helped me create meaningful relationships with my team members, our clients, and strategic partners, but there was a ceiling to my ability to get to deeper levels because I did not know myself well at all. While I had been in therapy since I was 16, I was stuck in selfhood and an identity of victimization. In business, I mastered the art of *confident assimilation*, but internally I couldn't see my way out from under the dark cloud that followed me. I felt so uncomfortable in my own skin, as if I didn't belong or fit in the way other people did. I had no idea the childhood trauma I experienced was abnormal, or that it was characterized as *complex* because multiple wounds occurred continuously over a long period of time.

## What Is Trauma, Anyway?

Greek in origin, the word *trauma* literally means "wound." If, as a child, you ever felt frightened, under threat, humiliated, abandoned, invalidated, unsafe, unsupported, trapped, ashamed, or powerless, then you have experienced trauma. Full stop. Events could have occurred once or been ongoing for years. They could have been a direct experience of suffering, or of witnessing of someone else's suffering. Simply living in a chaotic environment, or being impacted by dysfunction in your family or in the community to which you belonged, could have been traumatizing to your nervous system. If you believe you had a great childhood simply because you weren't abused and your parents stayed together, you might find the rest of this chapter eye-opening. If you know you experienced a very difficult childhood, this content is likely to resonate even more deeply for you.

> *"Trauma is not what happens to you. Trauma is what happens [within] you, as a result of what happens to you."*[3]

> **—Dr. Gabor Maté**
> *THE WISDOM OF TRAUMA*

When people talk about "big 'T' trauma," they're referring to Adverse Childhood Experiences (ACEs). ACEs can include experiencing physical or sexual abuse, neglect, or intimate partner violence; living with family members with mental health or substance abuse problems; or instability in relationships through parental separation or incarceration, to name a few.[4] These can also include significant suffering due to war or a natural disaster during childhood. If you find yourself scanning your own historical experiences, or if you're wondering just how common ACEs are, about 62% of adults surveyed in the United States reported experiencing at least one of these adversities during childhood. For socioeconomically and racially diverse populations, nearly 70% report at least one ACE.[5] Personally, I'd like to work on an updated ACEs survey since it's been about 30 years since the original, when very few people talked about trauma, and I posit that these numbers edge much closer to 100%. Not to mention that I believe some big "T" trauma is missing from the classification list.

What we know from studies on prolonged traumata is that post-traumatic stress disorder (PTSD) can be developed at any point in life due to a disruption in and alteration of brain chemistry. For those who suffer from PTSD, it can feel as though they relive traumatic events through flashbacks or situations that mimic detailed aspects of those events. Often, trauma survivors have trouble sleeping, constantly assess potential threats, and avoid reminders of their experience. This state of being makes it difficult to function in social settings, such as work environments, friend groups, family gatherings, and intimate relationships.[6]

Approximately 20% of people who report experiencing a traumatic event go on to develop PTSD, and approximately 8.7% of all adults—one in 13 people—will develop PTSD at some point during their lifetime.[7] When "big 'T'" adversities are compounded—when someone experiences chronic trauma over months or years—PTSD can become complex posttraumatic stress disorder, or CPTSD.

Other types of traumatic experiences—essentially when our basic physiological or emotional needs went unmet in childhood—are the result of events that exceeded our capacity to cope and caused a disruption in emotional function, and are sometimes called "small 't' trauma." As Elyssa Barbash explains, "These distressing events are not inherently life or bodily-integrity threatening, but perhaps better described as ego-threatening due to the individual left feeling notably helplessness. One of the most overlooked aspects of small 't' traumas is their accumulated effect. While one might not lead to significant distress, multiple or compounded small 't' traumas, particularly within a short span of time, are more likely to lead to an increase in distress and trouble with emotional functioning."[8]

Business coach and mindset therapist Nicole Lewis-Keeber encapsulates it best: "Big 'T' trauma explodes and little 't' trauma erodes, but they are both powerful enough to move a mountain."[9]

Another form of trauma that many of us have experienced, especially as adults within our workplaces, places of worship, or other institutions, is *systemic trauma*. The policies of environments or institutions can directly or indirectly harm individuals or particular populations. That could be financially, mentally, emotionally, physically, sexually, or spiritually.[10] Systemic issues, such as food scarcity, poverty, poor healthcare, and under-resourced education often give rise to trauma due to the contextual conditions they create.

*Organizational trauma*, a subset of systemic trauma, is when policies, practices, or the demands of work delivery itself causes suffering among a workplace's people and culture.[11] It "can stem from a single event, like a workplace violence incident or the sudden death or departure of a longtime leader. It can stem from long-term exposure to an intense stressor like a pandemic or secondary traumatization from working with trauma survivors. Or, it can emerge from a buildup of damaging patterns in how management and leadership relate to each other," explains Rachel Sam of Nonprofit Risk Management Center.[12] Most commonly, organizational trauma is seen in toxic work environments where employees are exploited, excluded, and/or denied opportunity based on race, ethnicity, citizenship, social class, age, gender, sexual orientation, religion, and disability. This is pervasive throughout all sectors, from nonprofits and government agencies to small businesses and corporations alike.

What are the fallouts for an organization that inflicts trauma on its workforce? Research in traumatology suggests that workplaces experience both direct and cumulative negative effects, such as poor customer relations; deterioration in quality of product or service; detachment from collaboration and cooperation; inability to solve both internal and external challenges; loss of trustworthiness of, and loyalty to, leadership; and transformation of an open culture to one of overwhelm.[13]

Particularly in the healthcare, psychotherapy, human services, and emergency services professions, *vicarious trauma* is also prevalent. Alternatively called *compassion fatigue*, secondary trauma is a natural but disruptive by-product of working with trauma survivors and traumatized clientele.[14] These professionals might face intense situations on a daily basis that impact them on all levels, and sometimes activate emotional wounds due to the similarity of past experiences.

*Collective trauma* is a devastating, shared occurrence that impacts a specific group of people, an entire population, or society at large. Beyond the historical event itself, the tragedy is embedded in the group's recollective memory—both to reproduce and to reconstruct the sequence of events in an effort to analyze it. Collective victimization also impacts those who might be distanced from the traumatic event(s) by time and/or space.[15] Some examples include slavery in America; the Holocaust; the atomic bombings of Hiroshima and Nagasaki; the attack on Pearl Harbor; the assassinations of John F. Kennedy, Dr. Martin Luther King Jr., and Malcolm X; the massacres at Columbine High School and Sandy Hook Elementary School; 9/11; the murder of George Floyd; the COVID-19 pandemic; and the Israel-Hamas war.

*Generational trauma* is a subconscious and/or genetic transmission of adverse experiences on generations or cultural groups that have a history of systemic oppression. Some examples include colonization, slavery, racism, discrimination, genocide, misogyny, war, community violence, natural disasters, famine, pandemics, recession, and acts of terrorism. In transferring experiences, the respective lineage of people's thoughts, feelings, and behaviors are influenced by the originating trauma.

*Intergenerational, multigenerational,* or *transgenerational trauma* is typically relegated to trauma passed down among familial relations but can also be observed on a societal level. This might begin with an event affecting one individual or multiple events affecting multiple family members. So we literally pass down our traumatic experiences from one generation to the next. In terms of continuance or mitigation, when we don't open up and work through the trauma we experienced, its detrimental cycle of impact continues. When we bring our psychological wounds into the light, we have the ability to heal and integrate for the benefit of future generations. All it takes is one person to stop the repetition.

## Trigger Warning

Today, the word *triggered* refers to the experience of having an emotional reaction to disturbing content, being around someone who reminds us of a past trauma, or feeling a strong sensory connection to a traumatic event—also referred to as *traumatic coupling*. While researchers don't know precisely how triggers are formed, some believe that the part of our brains that stores memories treat traumatic events differently from nontraumatic events. Since the brain cannot distinguish between a current and a past experience, triggers can cause a seemingly inexplicable emotional reaction well before we realize what might be underneath our reaction.[16]

I personally choose not to use the term *triggered* because I'm mindful to use trauma-informed language that doesn't negatively impact those who have served in the military or experienced gun violence in any form—such as hijacking, domestic abuse, school or other mass shootings, having a friend or family member die by gun suicide,

or unintentional death or injury. Instead, I prefer to say *activated,*
*reminded,* or *notified* to denote the experiences of those with PTSD or
CPTSD. Use the language that feels right for you.

In the context of healing and integration, many of us hold the
belief that we haven't healed yet because we still experience activating
effects. Human connection specialist Mark Groves offers an important
consideration: "Healing isn't about getting rid of triggers; it's about
changing what we do with them. We don't want to remove triggers;
they are warning signs, alerts in our bodies that similar circumstances
have led to pain, suffering, disconnection. Triggers are an invitation
to pay attention. Healing is what we do with the triggers; instead of
reacting to them, we respond to them."[17]

## Reactions to Trauma

Since trauma lives in the body, it can provoke the nervous system
years into adulthood, or even for an entire lifetime for some. That
remembrance sends us into the depths of trauma reactions like *fight,*
*flight, freeze,* or *fawn* (or *faint*). Trauma specialist Pete Walker explains,
"Polarization to a [4Fs] response is not only the developing child's
unconscious attempt to obviate danger, but also a strategy to purchase
some illusion or modicum of attachment."[18]

My freezing as an adult was simply a response to the trauma
that still lived in my body, and it was easily activated by any verbal conflict, regardless of its level of significance to others. People
didn't have a clue that when they raised their voice even in the
slightest, it threw me right back into my younger years where my
mother would scream hysterically and then physically hurt me. As
an adult, it appeared to others that I was uninterested or zoned
out, but inside I was frozen with fear. My intake of the situation as
an adult did not match up with reality: we were simply trying to
resolve a misalignment through conversation, but I froze as a means
of self-preservation.

So how do we develop mechanisms so early in life to cope with
traumatic experiences, and what determines the trauma reaction we
tend toward? Our nervous system becomes dysregulated when over-
whelmed; when that happens, we enter a state of fight, flight, freeze, or

fawn. Diving a little deeper, these involuntary physiological changes occur in the brain and body when there is a perceived threat, risk, or stress. Keep in mind that these responses are natural and designed to make us find safety by combating, fleeing, or shutting down in the face of what we feel might be dangerous. Part of our animal-body wiring, they are initiated upon our first exposure to a negative situation or experience, and our response develops over time as we encounter similar events.

## Fight

Many people who go into *fight* were abused, belittled, or completely ignored or neglected in childhood. Their responses—from yelling and screaming to becoming defensive, aggressive, or bullying—are motivated by the subconscious commitment never to repeat those prior experiences.[19]

## Flight

Those who go into *flight*—a reaction to a constant perception of danger—are often anxious and distance themselves through workaholism, perfectionism, and overplanning. An acute stress response causes the body's sympathetic nervous system to react by increasing heart rate, breathing, and oxygen flow to your major muscles while decreasing digestion.[20]

## Freeze

Flight-on-hold, a *freeze* response, provides time for the brain to decide how to respond and reduces the impact of the event through dissociation. While dissociation occurs a bit in all four responses, it's likely the strongest for those with a freeze response, also known as the *camouflage response*.[21] Dissociation is a simultaneous dichotomy of knowing and not knowing during an intolerant amount of stress.[22] In the body, though, the nervous system remains on high alert nearly all the time.

## Fawn

The *fawn* response is commonly associated with people-pleasing or appeasing in order to avoid conflict. Those who grew up in unpredictable homes became hypervigilant and adapted easily to create some modicum of safety by catering to every demand or request as a means of self-protection.[23]

These ingenious human adaptations have evolved. Threat perception and the need for safety were paramount when we hunted and gathered all of our food. Our senses had to be on high alert if we wanted to return to our village with bounty. Fast-forward and our threat perception is in overdrive because we're constantly scanning for physical danger as much as we're protecting ourselves from verbal, mental, and emotional hazards. Ideally, though, we would be able to access the healthy, necessary aspects of all four types of trauma responses.

"If the fight/flight/freeze response is successful and we escape the danger, we recover our internal equilibrium and gradually 'regain our senses.' If for some reason the normal response is blocked—for example, when people are held down, trapped or otherwise prevented from taking effective action . . . the brain keeps secreting stress chemicals, and the brain's electrical circuits continue to fire in vain," explains Bessel van der Kolk. "Long after the actual event has passed, the brain may keep sending signals to the body to escape a threat that no longer exists."[24]

This explains why we get activated when encountering a situation or person that reminds us of a traumatic event or experience, even years or decades after an initial occurrence. Traumatic experiences might affect self-awareness by creating barriers to the recognition and effective processing of emotions, which can hinder conscious leadership development.

## Epigenetics and Leadership

Epigenetics, a relatively new biological field of study, explains the likely inheritance of trauma to subsequent generations of those who experienced it firsthand.[25] Research suggests that trauma can impact the activity of DNA segments in a person, which can also influence whether genes for certain traits and diseases are turned on or off.[26] According to

Sol Davidson and Dr. Paul Brown, "the switching on and off of these RNA-based sub-structures of the DNA is known as *epigenetic change—* or *social* or *perceptual epigenetics*. This differentiates it from *molecular epigenetics*, which is the detailed understanding of exactly what proteins and neurochemicals are at play in the DNA/RNA bond."[27] Let's dig into social epigenetics a little further because it's a conversation I have yet to encounter with anyone beyond the handful of academics, clinicians, and coaches working in the fields of trauma and leadership.

Emerging neuroscience research shows how continuous trauma throughout childhood can lead to a shutdown of the genetic capacity to produce the hormones required for empathy, compassion, relationships, a sense of connectedness, and belonging. If that leaves the genetic structure to produce only adrenaline and cortisol, the implication is that some leaders could be *locked into operating unconsciously* from a place of threat perception. The consequences are startling when they are charged with making decisions that impact entire organizations, states, and countries.

Adrenaline and cortisol production is a crucial part of the evolutionary need to create adaptive and survival responses in children. If, however, the level of stress and trauma continues throughout childhood up to early adolescence, this can disproportionately produce copious amounts of adrenaline and cortisol as the child's normal baseline for all actions. Coupled with little to no demand from the environment for dopamine and serotonin, behavior can be dominated and characterized by high levels of fear, anger, aggression, splitting, depression, and drive—with little or no balancing interpersonal, relational, or constructive human skills. This then becomes the individual's standard method of functioning in adult life.

I find epigenetic change within some of the most domineering political and business leaders fascinating. It seems textbook when it's played out for the world to observe, though not many people seem to ask *why* these leaders behave the way they do—and why so many people follow and vote for them. Sol Davidson and Dr. Brown provided insight in a recent email exchange:

> Perhaps it is no small wonder that leadership in the U.S. and UK is showing signs of decline on the world's socio-political and

economic stage, especially as such a significant percentage of these countries' populations appear to be subject to adrenaline/cortisol and dopamine/serotonin (AC/DS) hormonal imbalance. This could well start to account for the political surge towards aggressive, populist, right-wing extremist political leadership in both the U.S. and Europe as AC/DS-unbalanced individuals who become visible as leaders unconsciously resonate with and are endorsed by constituencies also characterized by similar levels of hormonal AC/DS imbalance.

Reviewing the early childhood and family of origin dynamics of leaders such as Vladimir Putin, Donald Trump, Boris Johnson, the Koch Brothers, Josef Stalin, Adolf Hitler, and Elon Musk, published material shows that each experienced traumatic, violent, unstable, and unpredictable family-of-origin and extended early life trauma. Given these backgrounds, it would appear that AC/DS imbalance most likely occurred for these individuals and can go a long way in explaining their toxic, dysfunctional, aggressive, and dissociative behaviors, lacking in, or void of, the more humane qualities of empathy, compassion, or relatedness.

Such hormonal imbalances do not necessarily always lead to toxic and dysfunctional leadership but can lead to high levels of success by societal measurement. Such is the case with leaders like Jeff Bezos, and Ronald Reagan, both of whom had traumatic, disturbed, and turbulent childhoods. The resultant AC/DS imbalance, however, might have led to excessive and obsessive work hours and a relentless and aggressively focused determination for achievement and public recognition instead.[28]

## Unintegrated Information

Given the various experiences of trauma that individuals can experience, the most holistic definition I've come across is simply *unintegrated information* or an *unintegrated resource*, per the work of Steve Hoskinson, founder of the Organic Intelligence Outreach Institute.[29] This definition resonates with me because it transmutes the focus from what happened to us to how we will reclaim our power by using what we learned to better understand ourselves and empathize with others.

As we heal, the bedrock of who we know ourselves to be gets stronger. From that place, the need to defend or react in wounded ways falls away. We become more mature and can more easily decide how we desire to respond to stimuli. The difference is that we actively and easefully choose.[30]

While the path of information integration is certainly not linear—and we'll get into the *Spiral of Healing* in Part III—my experience is that it's entirely possible to amalgamate even prolonged trauma. Through willingness, observation, rest, and continual practice, I've gained insight into how the physical and emotional abuse I experienced has impacted my mindset, feelings, and behaviors. Beyond insight, I've developed a keen sense of awareness when someone or something activates my early history. From there, I can choose to think, speak, or act differently, with a higher level of consciousness for myself and others.

## Getting It Right

Regardless of what your own personal brand of trauma looked like, or when impactful incidents occurred, it's important to accept that the past cannot be changed, nor was any of what you experienced your fault. These experiences have manifested as psychological wounds and maladaptive behaviors. The gap in effective leadership is bridging the work of healing with how we consciously lead others.

There is no right or wrong way to process, progress, and transform one's self, which is a very important foundation, given that many leaders suffer from perfectionism and are motivated by *getting it right*. Who, me?

The journey from healing your past wounds to becoming a conscious leader is unique to every individual. You chart your own course. My core wound will be different from yours, even if we experienced the exact same traumatic event(s). There might have been a singular situation in your youth that informs much of your behavior as a leader, or perhaps your trauma was a compounded series of memories that only reinforced your *not-good-enough* story.

I see my role as preparing you for the inevitable resistance and setbacks that you will encounter on your healing journey. You'll know you're doing well every time you notice resistance and continue anyway, or whenever you take three steps forward and two steps back. Accepting that cadence is part of the process; there is no accelerant here.

*"In today's America, we tend to think of healing as something binary: either we're broken or we're healed from that brokenness. But that's not how healing operates, and it's almost never how human growth works. More often, healing and growth take place on a continuum, with innumerable points between utter brokenness and total health."*[31]

**—Resmaa Menakem**
*MY GRANDMOTHER'S HANDS*

Now that we know what trauma is, we'll briefly get into the differences between maintaining our psychological health and integrating our trauma. What I'd like to leave you with here is that this journey is all your own. So long as you remain open and committed to learning, understanding, and loving yourself, the path will seemingly unfold before you. Your deep knowing will guide you in the direction that will be most beneficial, even if dark or painful at times. The beautiful work you're doing for yourself will also positively impact everyone else who experiences the fully integrated version of you.

# 6

## Maintenance Versus Healing

BEFORE WE GET into the four fundamentals and I share more of my story with you, I want to surface the bifurcation between *mental health maintenance* and *trauma integration modalities*.

Please read this chapter three times before you decide to get offended by what I'm bringing to light for further consideration and conversation. Mental health maintenance does not address the wounds that are at the core of our composition. The kinds of modalities I'm talking about here are those I've experienced myself. You might be surprised to see some of the very therapeutic techniques or processes that you might have used, or currently engage with, as well. And if you are using any of the following so-called healing modalities as *subconscious avoidance* or a *coping mechanism*, just be aware that their usage can prohibit the true integration of your trauma. My experience is that these maintenance methods have been useful in setting me on a path toward healing, but they did not function as trauma integration modalities. This is also backed by research studies and the foremost experts in the field, such as Gabor Maté, Bessel van der Kolk, Resmaa Menakem, E. Kitch Childs, Hope Landrine, Linda James Myers, Babette Rothschild, Janina Fisher, Pat Ogden, Stephen Porges, Peter Levine, Deb Dana, Bruce Perry, and Daniel Siegel, to name a few.

With the emergence of somatic healing practices—those that help your body understand that the trauma is over and no longer needs to perceive associations as threat—we now have effective alternatives that are making their way into the mainstream. My goal here is to make the distinction between these types of modalities so you keep your gaze at the horizon, and constantly ask yourself which next step is right for you.

## Talk Therapy

Cognitive behavioral therapy (CBT) might help us verbally process what we might not be able to tell peers, family members, or coworkers. It can be an incredibly useful first step, and there might certainly be aha moments that arise over the course of time with a good therapist. However, there are also some inherent issues with talk therapy that work against the integration of trauma.

First, the two primary roles of traditional psychotherapy are to "evaluate, diagnose and treat a patient's behavioral dysfunctions resulting from, or related to physical and mental health,"[1] as well as to manage chronic illness. This recollection model is quite different from moving trauma out of the body—to heal and integrate that emotional history into the fabric of one's conscious awareness.

Critics of CBT also argue that because its primary charge is to address acute problems that are currently top-of-mind for the patient, such as being in a tumultuous relationship, it does not thoroughly uproot the underlying causes of those issues.[2] Others argue that if a big "T" trauma is discussed, the exposure-based approach is focused on the event itself. Some therapists believe that having patients recall traumatic events in great detail serves to desensitize them from the emotional pain by inspecting events from all angles. In reality, that approach isolates incidents along the timeline of your past, as if your emotional response to the event were not part of a series in a chain of events. Not only can repeated recollection exhaust and/or numb the person from accessing the spectrum of human emotion, but CBT typically requires months or years to make progress—while the trauma remains unprocessed in the body.[3]

Lastly, CBT does not typically attempt to bring generational or systemic issues into the fold, which often have a tremendous impact on one's mental health and overall engagement with life.[4]

Bessel van der Kolk echoes these views and adds, "For a hundred years or more every textbook of psychology and psychotherapy has advised that some method of talking about distressing feelings can resolve them. However, as we've seen, the experience of trauma itself gets in the way of being able to do that. No matter how much insight and understanding we develop, the rational brain is basically impotent to talk the emotional brain out of its own reality."[5]

To be clear, I'm a proponent of CBT—as a first step on the path. Starting at 16, I found therapy to be an ideal entrance into giving voice to what was happening inside my home and my head. I did, however, find myself frustrated by a desire for something more. There can be a knowing that your emotional stuckness needs to be interrupted or purged somehow. That the brain needs to be *rewired* so that the body's response to associative experiences can begin to change.

## Remedial Coaching

You might wonder why I, as a coach myself, would include coaching under the umbrella of *ineffective for trauma integration*. The devil is always in the details. Remedial coaching, also called *behavioral coaching*, has a clear and strong orientation toward solution. The idea that something is broken or wrong with one's behaviors insinuates that an external fix is needed to remove or cease that behavior. Justin Foster encapsulates this as *monetized codependency*.

Inherently, the break-fix lens through which remedial coaches view their clients creates a dynamic in which the client is unable to come to their own conclusions or make decisions based on what they truly desire. Clients are set up to rely on their behavioral coach to advise them on next steps, which is more akin to a consulting relationship.

The antithesis of remedial coaching would be variations of shadow work, inner child healing, somatic emotional therapy, and trauma-informed coaching. In these containers, coaches view their clients as the subject matter experts of their own lives. We hold space and offer contemplative questions—what Dr. Maté terms Compassionate Inquiry™. Clients are then able to begin correlating their adult behaviors to traumatic experiences during youth or even adulthood, empowering them to release false narratives and decide how they want to live and lead before committing to making changes of their own design.

## Superficial Self-Care

I derive many positive benefits from naps, massages, and retreat experiences. A hot bath feels life-giving. Sitting in the sunlight, reading a book, or drinking a hot cup of tea can be really relaxing. Eating a healthy meal nourishes the body as much as the mind, especially when there are no distractions. These can soothe the soul and tend to one's need for reprieve. However, if we're focused on the integration of trauma, these don't reach the depths necessary to heal from a painful past because they act as a temporary salve. They can distract us from feeling our feelings. A glass of wine might feel like regulation sometimes, but it's just a numbing agent.

When self-care remains at the surface, we tend to choose the options that make our bodies feel safe and protected. While this is encouraged, a singular practice can limit us from behavioral modifications that would negate the need for a surface-level salve so often. Instead, a deeper range of self-care includes getting clear on what you will and will not accept from, or engage in, with others; saying no to requests and people who do not serve your highest good; setting healthy boundaries (no matter how confronting it might be for others); taking long walks to move your body (and move trauma through); and exploring our feelings by putting pen to paper. Such guardrails enable the nervous system to relax and we can engage in trauma integration modalities.

## (Spiritual) Bypassing

When mental health maintenance is presented as a healing tool, it is disingenuous and dangerous. While some self-ascribed gurus can offer a fleeting hopeful moment or help reframe a situation at hand, there are often underlying issues—and avoidance thereof can lean into *bypassing*. You can think of *spiritual bypassing* as compensation for confrontation—meaning that to avoid working on our psychological wounds and the painful feelings that come with them, we sidestep it in the name of rising above. Coined by John Welwood in 1984, "when we are spiritual bypassing, we often use the goal of awakening or liberation to rationalize what [is called] premature transcendence: trying to rise above the raw and messy side of our humanness before we have fully faced and made peace with it."[6] Much of this is immersed in white privilege, perhaps unbeknownst to some self-proclaimed gurus. Perhaps not.

What does bypassing look or sound like? There are at least a dozen examples, but here are the seven most common applications, which occur every day, in our own homes, workplaces, or devout spiritual communities themselves:

## 1. Detachment, Without Compassion

In Buddhism, nonattachment is a core principle; however, its meaning is often misunderstood and used by some as a form of spiritual bypassing. Detachment is really about a deep involvement in life without being attached to any particular outcome. Someone with this mindset understands that to flow easefully with life, we must respect how impermanent everything is within and around us.[7] Indifference is the opposite of *detached compassion*, where we allow those we care about to make their own decisions and live with the consequences, while loving them—in simple terms, *letting go*. Those who bypass misunderstand that to mean not caring, and they use detachment to justify their lack of care.

## 2. Anger Avoidance

Anger is a natural human emotion; however, we've been taught that not all emotions are welcome in society. In reality, we not only have permission to feel angry, disappointed, sad, or any other emotion on the difficult end of the spectrum, but bearing witness to whatever emotions arise is uncomfortable for many of us. When spiritual practices, such as meditation, are used to avoid or suppress healthy emotions, that bypassing can be detrimental to your mental and physical health.

### 3. Racial Color Blindness

When someone says that they don't see color because they see humanity as one collective race, it's dismissive of people of color and the reality we have lived in for the last 400 years. There is simply not equality or equity—from food to safety, healthcare to housing, education, employment opportunities; the list goes on. When we claim color blindness, we are simultaneously "choosing to not just see race or skin color, but also the racial disparities, inequities, history of violence and current trauma perpetuated within a racist society."[8]

### 4. Toxic Positivity

Toxic positivity is an extreme need to see the good in all situations and come across as happy regardless of how we actually feel. Within the process of denying our real feelings, we minimize and invalidate the full spectrum of genuine human emotions.[9] Have you ever said, "Everything happens for a reason"? What about "Try to stay positive," or "If I can do it, so can you!"? Most of us have uttered these phrases to ourselves or others. Nontoxic and acceptance phrases[10] sound more like, "How can I best support you?" "What are you feeling in your body?" "I'm listening," and "Everyone's story and abilities are different, and that's okay." Trying to transcend the emotions that arise with autonomic trauma response and remain positive is unhealthy and even dangerous; trauma integration is about processing, regulating, and adapting to life's natural ups and downs.

### 5. Resilience

The act of toughening up works against trauma integration by burying one's emotions even further down. Resilience becomes problematic when it overlaps with toxic positivity, in that adversity can be tolerated to a detrimental degree, without acceptance of negative feelings surrounding the hardship.[11] Rewarded in our culture, resilience is often included in accolades, but very few people talk about how it can reinforce low-conscious behavior, such as aggression as a means of emotional protection, inflexibility, and artificial ego inflation. When this happens, leaders become rigid and less emotional. We know that when leadership lacks self-awareness, employees and entire organizations suffer unnecessarily.[12]

## 6. Attraction/Manifestation

There is plenty of scientific research supporting the detection of vibration and its various applications in humans.[13] The vibrational frequencies emitted from our energy bodies can signal how healthy, happy, and grateful we are, or conversely, how unhealthy, sad, or angry we are.[14] So it would stand to reason that those frequencies would act like magnets to attract similar frequencies and repel their opposite. However, the Law of Attraction tells us that if we believe bad things will happen to us, we are correct. It also reinforces the notion that we can achieve without any practicality or action taken on our own behalf. For some people, the setup for failure and disappointment can contribute to lower self-esteem and negatively impact mental health.[15] It ignores "the systemic power structures that enable injustice and reinforces the human predicament of not feeling good enough."[16]

## 7. Religion

Although this is an incredibly sensitive topic, I would be remiss if I didn't mention that a growing number of churches, mosques, and synagogues are now offering therapeutic counseling for trauma. This type of counsel can be helpful, *or* this can be spiritual bypassing in its most convincing disguise. In the latter case, religion can be used as a means *not* to work on our psychological wounds, as well as gain absolution for the trauma-rooted destructive behavior in which many of us have engaged.

Maladaptation is deemed *sin* in Christianity, *yetzer hara* in Judaism,[17] and *mahāpāpa* or *Adharma* in Hinduism. There is a common theme: transgressions against the will of an almighty God cause feelings of guilt in the human that committed them. In Buddhism, the concept of sin doesn't really have a place since there is no belief in a personal God, however, the term *pāpa* (or *apuñña*) describes "evil elements that defile the mind and have a deadening effect on the psyche, making it difficult for its upliftment."[18] As opposed to processing and integrating the trauma that is at the root of these behaviors, some religious counselors and texts suggest absolution. When accomplished through penance, prayer, compassion, or anything else that focuses on forgiveness from God for a transgression—and usually a request to be restored in some way—the focus is outside of ourselves, requiring validation from a higher power.

I'm not suggesting that any religious or spiritual practices that you might hold are invalid in any way. I can say that *sole reliance on religion* will not allow you to integrate the psycho-emotional wounds that reside in your body. Healing requires more than just the mind, and repenting for wrongdoing keeps real behavioral change at a distance. Inevitably the same wounded patterns play on repeat.

In many of these everyday examples of bypassing, it's clear that as human beings we will do anything to avoid taking ownership of the behaviors we exhibit due to our unprocessed trauma. My hope is that we've been able to find some common ground. If you feel activated by any of what I've called *maintenance*, or if you bristled at the idea that something doesn't apply, get curious. Think to yourself, "Why is this causing resistance inside of me?" Or, "What about these mental health maintenance examples might be true for me?"

In the end, if you conclude that your situation with these doesn't apply, I'm okay with that. In fact, I'd invite you to reach out and tell me more. Modeling conversations or exchanges about differing perspectives is not only how we grow and evolve as individuals; it also sets an example for those we lead.

# 7

# What Is High-Conscious Leadership?

CAN WE AGREE that there are limitations to *leadership* as we have historically defined it?

Leaders are either elected from a small set of people; promoted to positions of power within organizations, groups, or systems; or we create chief executive roles for ourselves via entrepreneurial pursuit. Perhaps the person at the helm of a corporation or organization—or state, province, or country for that matter—should no longer be automatically ascribed the title of *leader*. After all, none of these contexts centers on the healthy, influential characteristics that would make others want to follow someone.

Why have we done this—assigned this designation to anyone who commands a group, organization, or region? We've all come to see or experience in our lives that the act of commanding, being authoritative, or dominating is quite the opposite of cogent leadership.

What role does character and ethics play? What about the level of emotional intelligence and ability to convene spaces where people feel safe to be themselves? How about impact on communities, the environment, or systemic issues for which we can facilitate betterment? It seems to me like a new definition or set of criteria might be required at this point. Michael Gelb and Raj Sisodia pose this question in their book *The Healing Organization: Awakening the Conscience of Business to*

*Help Save the World:* "As business leaders and human beings, how can we turn a blind eye to that suffering when we actually have the ability to do something about it?"[1]

Conscious leaders are unable to turn a blind eye. They lean into discomfort. They possess self-awareness and the ability to respond with intention and consideration. Their curiosity and empathy enable them to prioritize people, planet, and profit simultaneously. Passionate about ensuring that there is no needless suffering among their team members, they work to create lasting positive impact within their domains and for future generations. When we can look beyond ourselves to consider every facet of the impact of our decisions, that's high-conscious leadership.

Conscious leaders can easily recognize and assess when "their primary commitment is to being right, and when their primary commitment is to learning."[2] Essentially, unconscious leaders have not done the work required to unlearn their emotional stimulants, and conscious leaders have developed deep introspection and remain steadfast in their commitment to themselves and all other stakeholders.

Most leaders operate unconsciously because our primitive brain's default state is to scan for threats—whether those are physical, environmental, egoic, or otherwise. The fear response that ensues is rooted in survival and therefore appears defensive and reactionary. Leaders who are in survival mode lack capacity for the consideration of others; they do not have the emotional ability for collaboration or compassion when in a defensive posture. They simply lack self-worth and seek validation from external sources as a means to feel safe and secure.

If a leader can develop intricate self-awareness and unlearn imprinting from past emotional experiences, the opportunity to lead well becomes possible. In my experience, the *integration of their trauma* is what sets them apart as high-conscious leaders. And that is precisely what determines, at a core level, why they are the opposite of low-conscious leaders.

## An Extended Definition

In my view, *high-conscious leadership* is the practice by which a leader engages in a lifelong commitment to posttraumatic growth, models vulnerability and radical support as cultural norms, and breathes life back into our ecosystem. While the triple bottom line was a good start to giving earth a stakeholder's seat at the table, I think we've surpassed the timeline when *sustainability* can continue to be a primary focal point. What we've really meant is *to sustain humans* and there is no selfless gift back to the earth in that, is there? We need leaders who have bolder visions for restoration, regeneration, and reciprocity. We need leaders who believe in themselves enough to act upon those visions.

Though rare, high-conscious leaders are found across multiple sectors as well as within the realms of activism. They are the exquisite embodiment of contemplation and catalytic action. Historical examples include Albert Einstein, Dr. Martin Luther King Jr., Nelson Mandela, Maya Angelou, and Desmond Tutu. Present-day examples include Arlan Hamilton, Arianna Huffington, Tammy Duckworth, Greta Thunberg, Yvon Chouinard (Patagonia), Hamdi Ulukaya (Chobani, La Colombe), Leena Nair (Chanel), Safra Catz (Oracle), Ursula Burns (Xerox), Sophia Leonora Mendelsohn (SAP), Christiana Figueres (Global Optimism), Elizabeth Wathuti (Green Generation Initiative), Arman Anatürk (HackCapital), Peggy Liu (JUCCCE), Pia Heidenmark Cook (IKEA), Steve Pemberton (Workhuman), Laila Tarraf (Allbirds), Vandana Shiva (Navdanya), Malala Yousafzai, Rihanna, Barbara Corcoran, Oprah Winfrey, and Michelle Obama. By the way, it should not be lost on us that most of these high-conscious leaders are women and people of color. Typically those who have faced significant adversity early on, or who have come into the world on fire, coerce change.

## Leaders as Healers

Taking the inner work one step further to bring us back to healing organizations, one of the most beneficial facets of high-conscious leaders is that they themselves are healers. Author Nicholas Janni talks about this as a reparative act that must take place inside of us as leaders before it can happen within those under our guardianship. This is done to mend the distinct disconnect, fragmentation, and polarization between the energy of *being* and *doing*.[3]

I see this so clearly in my own evolution as a leader. When I once adopted masculine characteristics as a young CEO, the trauma healing work I was doing began to soften that rigidity and need for credit and control. My behavior and language shifted along with it. A lifelong steward of the environment, I transferred that care to my employees' experiences as well. By the end of my tenure running a digital marketing agency, I had edged closer to high-conscious leadership. However, not until leading my consultancy and then moving into coaching did I fully embrace the role of *leader as healer*. I took this quite literally. In 2023, I became a certified Level III practitioner in the Japanese healing art of Usui Reiki, a holistic practice that serves to restore harmony on the physical, emotional, mental, and spiritual levels, as well as those that might be unconscious.[4]

In one-on-one immersive experiences with clients—what I call *The Reset*—I blend trauma-informed coaching, somatic emotional release, and the architecture of their visionary contributions in the world. I end each of these half-day sessions with Reiki to harmonize and unblock any latent energy. Facilitating these profound breakthroughs is one of the ways in which I empower leaders to move beyond what's holding them back, hold space for all emotions, and help them integrate physical, mental, emotional, spiritual, and etheric shifts that occur during our half-day session together. In short, my path to high-conscious leadership translated into a 180-degree change in my work in the world. It has, quite literally, become a new way of being for me.

> "It is radical, even revolutionary, to take responsibility for healing the whole by beginning with myself. . . . To be [healing] in order to be a healer is transformational."[5]
>
> **—Gene Early, PhD**
> *SENIOR LEADERSHIP ADVISOR*

Healing is a lifelong journey, meaning there is no destination point when you arrive *healed*. The work of healing is to understand and work with the trauma you've experienced to see the beautiful truth of who you are and to live more easefully. We'll cover this in more depth in Chapter 9. What's important to know upfront is that there's always more to learn, unlearn, discover, repair, reclaim, and experience.

You can do much of the work on your own, and but at times you will undoubtedly need external support. Ultimately the path, pace, and extent to which each of us embraces trauma integration will be entirely our own. Perhaps it would be helpful to start with a baseline.

## True North: Unveiling Your Leadership Identity

Knowing your leadership identity is vital to unlocking your path forward. One way I work with my clients is to take what I call the True North quiz, which is available at **klcampbell.com/leadership**.

This identity quiz asks you to consider 20 "I" statements. For example, "I am mostly the same person at work as I am at home," "I trust myself to handle stress in healthy ways," and "I accept that failure is part of the learning process." As you read each one aloud or to yourself, reflect on whether they are most like you (5), least like you (1), or somewhere in between (4, 3, or 2). You're not meant to overthink it; just read, feel, and respond. Be honest with yourself. If you have trouble with any of the statements, what body sensations do you notice when you read aloud? Or does a color come into your view if you close your eyes? If the sensation or color feels positive, your answer is likely true. If it feels negative, your response is likely false. Play with the prompts. Experiment with different ways of arriving at your answers. There is no right or wrong way; there is only your truth. What matters is that you're honest with yourself about these statements. Once you've ascribed a number to each statement online, the numbers will be totaled automatically, you'll receive your full results via email, and you will find out which type of leader you are.

Let's pause here for a moment to reflect on where you might go from here with this self-assessment.

> Once you've taken the leadership identity quiz, can you begin to correlate past experiences with your answers?
>
> What might it feel like to be a high-conscious leader—to be able to confidently mark all of these statements at a 4 or 5?

# 8

## Four Fundamentals

OTHER THAN A good amount of risk tolerance, the drive to prove oneself, and the ability to increase revenue year over year, no one ever tells us how to lead effectively, let alone what to expect along the way. There is no toolkit or manual for leading organizations. And there has been a marked lack of research, resources, and tools to help integrate the trauma we bring with us into our leadership roles.

We need a radical alternative to the rinse-and-repeat mentality we've all been led to believe—no, lied to believe—is necessary: to hustle, grind, crush, extract, command, control, produce, mask, suppress, and please. In the name of leading from a healthier, more secure place, I believe doing the difficult work of integrating our underlying trauma is the way forward. The path looks different for each and every one of us, yet the objective is similar for most of us: learn to regulate our emotions so we can respond versus react, create safety for ourselves, and set healthy boundaries in all areas of our lives. From here, all things become possible.

As leaders, we have a responsibility to work on our own emotional maturity in order to serve others from a place of integrity. The four fundamentals of high-conscious leadership are universal principles that I propose as a new framework for leading, living, and loving in the world today:

1. Integrating Trauma
2. Embodying Vulnerability

3. Leading with Compassion

4. Lighting the Way

I see the integration of childhood trauma, the modeling of vulnerability, having compassionate empathy, and raising others up as interconnected and inseparable fundamentals. In the final four parts of this book, I'll walk you through the overarching premise of the fundamentals. We'll explore the intrinsic, extrinsic, and systemic facets of each. I'll also share poignant vignettes and stories from my past because I want you to clearly see the correlations that might exist in your own story—and what the future is holding for you, too. I want you to know what values you prioritize most in the world. I want you to get clear—really clear—about who you are on a soul level, how your unique gifts were formed early on, and how to lead with higher consciousness for the rest of your life.

> "To transform business as a force for good, we need bold and brave leaders—individuals that are not afraid to get personal, emotional, and to define and defend their values."[1]
>
> —Lucy von Sturmer
> INITIATOR AND CHAIRPERSON, CREATIVES FOR
> CLIMATE; FOUNDER, THE HUMBLEBRAG

## Creating Healing Spaces

"Healing is a restorative, transformative process designed to return an organism back to health from an unbalanced, damaged or unervated condition while also strengthening the organism."[2] When we focus on our own transformative inner work, the way we see ourselves, others, and the world shifts in tandem. High-conscious leadership extends well beyond ourselves and how we treat others within our organization. The level of freedom we create for ourselves flows into the places we convene so others can not only exist in safe places but can be allowed to heal as well.

The act of healing represents an ongoing journey with many possible paths, as opposed to a destination in which a particular condition is considered *cured*.³ Since the pandemic, we have seen that many people no longer consent to being on the receiving end of repeated actions and damaging decisions made by leadership. Radical shifts are being made inside some organizations, disrupting or modifying systems and processes toward more inclusive, equitable solutions. Within workplaces, examples of the end-to-end processes being (or in need of being) overhauled include candidate recruitment, promotion to leadership, performance evaluations, change management, number of working hours/days per week and flex time, hybrid and work-from-home options, and breadth of benefits for all employees. This, too, has a name.

"*Organizational healing* refers to the work of repairing practices, routines, and structures in the face of disruption and strengthening organizational functioning through social relationships."⁴ Raj Sisodia says, "The premise . . . is simple: when we understand and meet people's *real* needs, we help to heal them, while healing ourselves and generating abundance. Conversely, when we uncover and prey on their cravings, desires, fears, and addictions, we hurt them, and ultimately we hurt ourselves, our children, and our planet."⁵

Research by Larissa Winter on the psychological effects of organizational trauma found that "in cases of severe adversity and high levels of conflict, the breadth of resources provided by an organization are as important as the speed of delivery of these resources to the employees." Winter continues:

> Successful organizational trauma support means compassion and comfort delivered by companies to their staff, in order to heal gradually and prevent potential retraumatization. The costs of hiring a team of grief counselors for a certain period of time are generally lower than the negative effects of employees not being supported adequately: lower performance levels, lower standards of customer service, increasing error-proneness and costly error rates, decreasing levels of employee loyalty towards the company, and potential multiplier effects regarding negative communication can generally be associated with higher costs in the long term.⁶

Research on organizational healing from over a decade ago focused on how colleagues under the same employer could help each other heal after a major natural disaster, severe technological failures, or industry-wide crisis, such as those in the financial sector during and following economic collapse.[7] The organizational healing I'm referring to is in response to trauma that has been created by prior or current leadership itself, including the structures and systems that leaders have put in place.

The adversities are usually small at first. The consistency with which they occur creates a compounding effect. "Traumatic events can be described as an accumulation of small and medium-sized mistakes, overlooked minor problems, unsafe acts and shortcomings" on the part of those in positions of power.[8] Uncertainty arises from unclear responsibilities, and insufficiently defined roles contribute to emotional exhaustion on the part of employees. If we are unaware and hyper-focused on growth, it seems like we turn around one day and suddenly everyone within our organization is at capacity and performance or product delivery is suffering. No—it is our people who are suffering, and we need to take responsibility for our part in both causing and allowing it to continue.

## Trauma-Informed Work Environments

In a trauma-informed workplace, leaders learn to identify individual and organizational suffering. Starting with an understanding of our own emotional history, we're also educated on anti-racism and inclusive, empathetic, and conscious leadership practices. From there, we get vulnerable by addressing the harm that has taken place, and we begin the work of healing it. With intentionality, commitment, and care, the organization can become a workplace where team members see and hear themselves and each other, and recognize the essential role they all play in the mission. Sound utopian? All it takes is willingness: employees willing to speak up, set boundaries, and advocate for themselves—and leaders willing to listen, commit, and implement. If everyone is working toward the same purpose, the metrics by which we measure success must include eco-reciprocity, psychological safety for all, and fiscal sustainability.

In Chapter 4, I explained why healing and high-conscious leadership matter more than ever before. What I want you to consider now, though, is why we exist. Existential stuff, I know. But really, how do we end up in the fields of work that we do? Why do we choose to be in relationship with the partners that we do? Why do we enlist the help of the other people we do?

*What if we do it all for the purpose of healing*—ourselves, each other, and the earth?

From conscious capitalism and diversity mandates for publicly traded companies to environmental commitments on the part of countries, there is a generative throughline between these and high-conscious leadership. The four fundamentals are at the heart of healing—our wounds, the natural resources we mistake as our own, and our relationship to money. As leaders, we engage in this practice because we know we were meant for something bigger than ourselves. It is that calling that only you can hear, that only you can feel in your body. And within your body is where we start. That is where trauma is trapped.

Nevertheless, real leadership starts with transforming our relationship to, and with, ourselves. The healing process begets vulnerability, which we can embody and model for others wherever we go. Our own practice with being vulnerable, coupled with the vulnerability we get to witness in others, augments our ability to lead with empathy for others' experiences. This healing circles back to our purpose—to light the way for everyone and everything to thrive.

This is the return to our True Nature: to live, lead, and love with an understanding that there is no self separate from anything else in the universe. You are me, and I am you. Neither of us is actually separate from those who we have been taught to believe are so different from us. Our souls understand this. We do the work for ourselves, which means we're doing the work for the benefit of others, and a regenerative cycle is born. High-conscious leaders understand this, and the win-win-win fuels their desire to deepen their knowledge, connection, and impact.

If there is one particular change in your behavior that you're eager to make, what is it?

How might your leadership style shift once you begin to develop deeper self-awareness—and what impact do you think it could have on others?

# PART

# When the Past Is Present

*"The soul always knows what to do to heal itself. The challenge is to silence the mind."*[1]

—Caroline Myss
AUTHOR

WHEN WE FEEL, speak, and act, the past is always present. In almost every case, whether we can recognize it or not, we are all carrying some form of deep pain. Why would that evaporate when we step into a leadership role? In fact, leaders are often in the spotlight, which means that what others might deem character flaws are made even more obvious under pressure.

Those so-called flaws are often rooted in textbook responses to childhood trauma. Addressing our core wounds and integrating them to the point that we can release attachment to them—when we can finally see and stop our repetitive, unhealthy patterns—is the key to unlocking our aptitude. I'm fascinated by the paradoxes and correlation between past trauma and how we lead.

So, how do we transmute deeply embedded mindsets like "I'll get them before they get me, or "I'll make them see how good I am"? Make no mistake that deep, ongoing work is required. Becoming introspective doesn't happen overnight; there are layers to sift through and sort out.

Various parts of your current identity might need to be dismantled, and that will undoubtedly be more than just a little uncomfortable.

When we do the work of healing, we take emotional responsibility for ourselves and how we move throughout the world, what we magnetize, and how we contribute our gifts. If you scoff at the idea that you have *gifts*—meaning that some of the strategies you implored to survive your childhood could be the basis of your leadership superpowers—prepare to be mind-blown. This is likely to be one of those before and after experiences. In fact, what you do after reading these next four chapters might be some of the most transformative work you've ever done in your life.

Again, go slow. Your nervous system will thank you, and you'll be demonstrating to yourself what real self-care looks like. *I'm so proud of you already.*

# 9

---

# Fundamental #1:
# Integrating Trauma

TALKING ABOUT TRAUMATIC experiences from childhood can be incredibly confronting. Many of us cannot yet see the bridge between our emotional challenges as adults and our childhood trauma. I would go so far as to say that the extent to which we've integrated our trauma might be the number one indicator of leadership efficacy.

> *"Traumatized people chronically feel unsafe inside their bodies: The past is alive in the form of gnawing interior discomfort. Their bodies are constantly bombarded by visceral warning signs, and, in an attempt to control these processes, they often become expert at ignoring their gut feelings and in numbing awareness of what is played out inside. They learn to hide from their selves."*[1]

> —**Bessel A. van der Kolk**
> *THE BODY KEEPS THE SCORE*

Historically, most people do not gravitate toward healing because it requires untold levels of courage to rise each day and challenge your own ego, work on the same issues over and over again, and feel everything while the majority of people seem blissfully numb. Actively healing and integrating our past might be the most painful and rewarding process we'll ever encounter in our lives. The most important of the four fundamentals—and the basis for this book—is that integrating the story of emotional wounds is the bedrock of becoming an effective leader.

## The Spiral of Healing

Using a spiral to describe the healing process is the most accurate vis-ual I can imagine. Trauma survivors can work through varying states of healing one or many times, in similar or seemingly random orders, using the same or completely different modalities. When a new behav-ioral response becomes available, we spiral in an upward direction, and the spiral becomes wider. Why? As we grow and heal, we gather new information about ourselves, greater access to both name and feel our emotions, a more robust suite of resources, more meaningful ways to care for ourselves, and the ability to modify our behaviors at the root level.[2]

The spiral of healing also implies that we are very likely to revisit the same issue multiple times, which means that it might often feel like we're sliding backward. I've often said, "I can't believe this is com-ing up again" or "I thought I was done with this!" Maybe you have, too. When you return to the same state multiple times, integration can feel discouraging.[3] The work of healing is ongoing, which means that the commitment is lifelong—and is most effective without an attach-ment to a particular time frame or destination.

The takeaway here is that integrating any big "T" or little "t" trauma is not a linear process. In fact, I prefer to talk about them as *states* instead of *stages* because there is little to no implication of a predetermined or progressive sequence. Physical wounds can heal in linear stages, but these wounds are far more complex, embedded in the psyche and body. Much of what we would like to heal might be com-pletely unknown to us, and the rest is what most of us prefer to avoid. So long as we are committed to healing for ourselves and the benefit of all our relationships, we will widen the spiral and continue moving upward and around.

In Chapter 11, I'll go deeper into the potential experiences you might have as you engage with the healing process. And I will reit-erate that trauma integration is nonlinear. In *The Myth of Normal,*

Dr. Gabor Maté and his son Daniel Maté remind us so beautifully of this truth: "No one can plot somebody else's course of healing because that's not how healing works. There are no road maps for something that must find its own individual arc. We can, however, sketch out the territory, describe it, familiarize ourselves with it, and prepare to meet its challenges. We can learn what natural laws seem to govern healing, specifically what attitudes and attributes it both awakens and responds to in us."[4]

## The Integration Tripod

If you're wondering what exactly is meant by *integration*, the following framework will offer more concrete comprehension. I think of the three components as a tripod holding up a camera: they work together to support your ability to capture where you are at any given moment.

### 1. Integration of the Story

Each one of us has a story—the *I'm not enough* or *I'm too much* stories that were implanted during our most formative time of life. We were just learning about our family systems, how things worked, and our place within the world. Somewhere along the way, others used unkind words, invalidated our experiences, and/or acted in ways that created the foundation of our core wound(s).

> **Acceptance:** Our responsibility as wiser adults is to parse out reality from the stories we were told about ourselves, and to view the thoughts that have calcified themselves in our psyche as just that. When we can see the situations, and words or actions of wounded people for what they were, we can begin to accept that they happened through no fault of our own. We can also begin to see ourselves as separate from our thoughts.
>
> With acceptance comes an understanding that our attempts to control or avoid the pain associated with our trauma might make it worse.[5] With acceptance comes the freedom to engage with life on our own terms. Integrating our previous narrative—allowing for any and all emotions to arise from it—with our new

story offers a new perspective. When we accept and embrace our feelings, we see clearly that *not only are we enough, but we are perfect as we are*.

What is one thing that you're working to accept right now?

## 2. Elimination of Self-Limiting Beliefs

If you believe you're broken, you'll stay on an eternal search for external healing. This is the derivation of the monetized codependency we covered in Chapter 6. There is a necessary set of fundamentals that can help you eliminate self-limiting beliefs, and neither requires an *ongoing* relationship with a therapist or guru. You have the innate wisdom for resourcing well and rewiring the neural pathways from negative self-talk to self-love.

**Rewiring:** The brain's lifelong ability to change to new inputs is known as *neuroplasticity*. During traumatic experiences, the thinking part of the brain goes offline, the amygdala gets activated, and then the nervous system responds. These autonomic responses—fight, flight, freeze, or fawn—are not thoughts; they are psychophysical reactions to an inability to regulate our emotions.[6]

More than two dozen studies have linked inflammation in the body of adults to mistreatment during childhood. Trauma-induced inflammation can impact the brain function of neurotransmission.[7] In the body, inflammation brings with it pain, discomfort, stiffness, and lack of flexibility and mobility.

So, between rewiring the brain and reducing inflammation, we can work toward eliminating the self-limiting beliefs that keep us stuck in situations, relationships, and jobs that thrive so long as we remain small, silent, and sans boundaries. You can use Freud's *reality testing* to change experiences that might be anxiety-inducing.[8] You can re-parent the younger version of yourself through *shadow work therapy* or *inner child healing*, which was one of my modalities of choice. You can use interventions like Eye Movement Desensitization and Reprocessing (EMDR) to alter how memories are stored in your brain by processing traumata without reliving them.[9] More of these kinds of modalities are on their way in Chapter 12.

What's one low-impact memory that you'd like to rewire in your brain? Why did you choose this specific memory?

**Self-Love:** The belief that being faster, smarter, stronger, or better would have prevented the trauma we experienced is incredibly common. Almost by default, we blame and shame ourselves to the point of self-criticism, self-hatred, and sometimes self-harm. Maybe you've spent more than half of your life in a perpetual loop of negative self-talk.

Loving yourself is antithetical to many of the messages you might have received or ingested during childhood, adolescence, and early in your career. That's why it's so damn hard to love yourself as part of the healing process, to love yourself to the core of your existence. Yet if you can unlock the mysterious key to life that is unconditional self-love, you can officially leave this simulation behind.

I used to think that self-love was for other people. I understood the concept on an intellectual level, but it seemed so untouchable. *How could I love myself when my own mother couldn't love me?* It wasn't until I could see myself through my own eyes—without the clouded lens of her familial wounds—set healthy boundaries, trust my intuition again, and re-parent my younger self that I began to form a loving relationship with myself. In a state like this, self-limitation can all but fall away, and when it does try to resurface—because the spiral of healing is real—I see it as an invitation to explore what more there is to heal.

Since it might be easier to name what you don't love about yourself, name two things that you do love.

Why do you love those things, and is there a way you could love them even more?

### 3. Regulation of Emotions

Just like "angry people live in angry bodies" and "hurt people hurt people," the opposite is true when we're actively integrating our trauma: "Healing people help heal people." (It's unclear who coined this phrase, but I did modify it from its original form, "Healed people heal people.") They do so by, for example, creating psychological safety and convening safe environments, inviting others who have undergone similar experiences to feel less alone, and mentoring people who struggle with the same issues. Some of us share the process, lessons, and healing journey in more public ways because we know it resonates.

## Self-Awareness

If self-awareness is knowing what emotions we're feeling and why we're feeling them, then emotional regulation is choosing how we respond to those emotions. As children, we learn the social rules; by adulthood, most of us understand how our emotions should be expressed or inhibited in all social settings.[10] Yet trauma complicates society's expectations of our emotional responses. Awareness of our own bodily sensations, brain activity, and the intensity and quality of our emotions—the totality of what's happening within our entire internal system—gets hijacked.

Being committed to healing and integrating our trauma typically starts with a desire to change. For most of my life, I was somewhat unaware of the visibility and impact that my emotional dysregulation and maladjusted behavior had on others. My level of discomfort became so great by my late thirties that the only option was drastic change in all aspects of my life. As I began making major shifts, my level of self-awareness bloomed in tandem. I noticed a deeper trust in myself and more cognizance of my impact on others—which was especially helpful when I needed to set boundaries with the very people who were most likely to activate me the most.

From 1–5, how would you rate your level of self-awareness, with 5 being the most self-aware?

## Behavioral Modification

Some scientists believe that 20% to 60% of behavior is genetically pre-determined.[11] However, it's more likely that nervous system responses due to childhood trauma, new genetic activation due to environmental upbringing, and epigenetics due to generational trauma—and, yes, genetic expression due to several other variables—combine to inform one's temperament. After all, not only can childhood trauma alter the structure of the brain but also it can modify the expression of genes that regulate stress, leading to an increased probability of anxiety and depression, as well as a decrease in the ability to regulate negative impulses.[12]

Once we become aware of any negative impact we have on others, we have a choice to commit to changing our behavior. Like most things that require hard work and support, it comes down to willingness. We can choose to continue treading in the maladaptive behavioral soup of today, or we can have agency over how we want to experience the rest of our life.

If I can change my behavior from a place of victimization, an anxious attachment style, and a core wound of not mattering, anyone can. And if you're not totally familiar with attachment styles, we'll be going in-depth on those.

> If you could change just one behavior that can be traced back to childhood trauma, which one would it be? How would you modify it?

The Integration Tripod offers a comprehensive framework for healing past trauma and transforming our lives. The three components— integration of the story through acceptance, elimination of self-limiting beliefs through rewiring and self-love, and regulation of emotions through self-awareness and behavioral modification—work together to support our journey of self-discovery and evolution. By engaging with these components in the name of integration, we can embark on a transformative journey that leads to self-acceptance, wholeness, and a more empowered and fulfilling life.

# 10

---

# Practicing Introspection

INTEGRATING TRAUMA BEGINS with *introspection*—the consistent practice of going inward to experience and understand your own thoughts, feelings, and behaviors. Self-reflection is a conscious awareness of one's holistic way of being in the world. It's honed mindfulness about the impact that you and your decisions have on all stakeholders: you and your family, those you lead and their families, shareholders, your clients or customers, your local community, and the natural environment.

Before anything else, deep introspection is necessary to understand the connection between who we are and how we show up as individuals and leaders. It is how we begin to develop self-awareness. This level of awareness goes well beyond the self; it allows for openness with others, curiosity about their experiences, and the ability to hold space and listen with intention. Look outside of what we've been fed for so long; get curious and remain open-minded.

As Gina Hayden puts it, "Since our ego at its strongest loves to become fixed on particular positions and to defend these as being right, conscious leaders model curiosity. . . . It's about suspending what you already know in order to make room for new ideas and perspectives to emerge. . . . We have to be willing to let go of all of our fixed ideas and look again."[1]

## Developing and Deepening Conscious Awareness

If letting go doesn't feel accessible just yet, perhaps you can experiment with holding your fixed ideas more lightly. With conscious awareness comes more choice. We can choose to be more inquisitive, to listen to others with the sole intent of understanding them, and to examine our own internal thoughts, feelings, and judgments. Each opportunity is part of developing self-awareness—the one thing that everyone agrees is a required characteristic of conscious leaders, but one that remains elusive because very few have offered *how*.

Many people also leverage the practice of meditation to deepen their conscious awareness. Meditation can lead to increased mindfulness, an awareness of our thoughts, and a state of higher consciousness. A greater sense of freedom becomes available when we actively engage in the process of allowing our thoughts to occur naturally, thanking them for their presence, and then releasing any attachment we might feel to them.

When we engage in a meditation practice over several years, we might experience our mind as less frenetic and less easily distracted. We might even find that our sensitivity is heightened when we engage in meaningful external activities. When we can find serenity, we have the opportunity to be enveloped in the present.[2] We can feel at one with everything around us. It's a profound tool that can become a way of being—and we're getting closer to the menu of modalities that I've compiled for you to explore.

## What's Your Attachment Style?

Since there are so many ways to do the work, let's start with one of the last ones on my list, attachment theory, since it's central to understanding our own trauma to re-parent our inner child.

In the early 1990s, Kim Bartholomew and Leonard M. Horowitz revealed a four-group model of attachment styles for adults that has generally been applied to personal relationships up to this point. The four groups of attachment types are *Secure, Anxious-Preoccupied, Dismissive-Avoidant,* and *Fearful-Avoidant,* also called *Disorganized.* Based on our relationship with one or both parents, we are likely to find the foundations of our particular attachment style in childhood.[3]

Becoming cognizant of your attachment style can help you understand why you behave the way you do in all types of relationships—at home, in social groups, and at work. Because of the particular coaching I do with leaders, I began to draw a correlation between the attachment style of the business owners and their reactions to myriad workplace situations. What I noticed was that those who were more secure had more sustainable companies. They walked away from new business if it wasn't a fit for the firm. Their employees reported feeling well-supported. If an issue arose with a partner, team member, or client, they worked to resolve those issues through productive conversations. They avoided making generalizations; they listened to understand (versus to reply); they communicated compassionately while still holding people accountable. And they set healthy boundaries, so they didn't suffer from overwhelm the way most other owners did.

Essentially, those with secure attachment styles were naturally more conscious leaders. Those with more anxious attachment styles presented as conscious leaders, but their people-pleasing tendencies ultimately created unhealthy workplace environments.

To be clear, very few people have an entirely secure attachment style. We all had needs that went unmet during our formative years, and we invented mechanisms and frameworks to help us feel safe and derive a sense of belonging. Again, those were brilliantly designed strategies that helped us survive our environment early on, but many of those end up being the very things that keep us from thriving as adult leaders.

The good news is that attachment styles can and do change as we evolve. In fact, most of us will have experienced all four styles throughout our lives. When we become aware of them, we have the opportunity to change our thoughts, language, and behaviors. I believe that it is our responsibility to consciously evolve beyond the primary attachment style we developed in youth. In business, understanding your style might help you understand why you have a hard time closing a sale or managing specific team members. I'll break down what you can do about it, but first let's dive into the four different relational attachment styles.

**Anxious-Preoccupied:** Those who tend to feel more nervous about relationships and are more likely to be needy or jealous are Anxious-Preoccupied.[4] They often go to a worst-case scenario when evaluating someone's intentions or words. There is also a need for ongoing validation and expressions of acceptance.

If you're *Anxious-Preoccupied*, you might come across as desperate when trying to win new business. If someone criticizes your work, you might get defensive or withdraw from dealing with the critic. You might obsess over the tiny details of your latest interaction, and fret about layers of meaning in what someone said—which might or might not exist.

**Dismissive-Avoidant:** Freedom-loving and self-sufficient, people who have a Dismissive-Avoidant style are likely to avoid intimacy because they don't want to be vulnerable. They put work and other activities before their relationships because closeness and commitment are difficult for them.

If you're *Dismissive-Avoidant*, you might have trouble attracting new business because you struggle with the empathy, inclusion, and consciousness that customers today want to see. Since vulnerability is a key to influential leadership, you might also notice a disconnect between you and the people under your stewardship.

**Fearful-Avoidant/Disorganized:** People who are Fearful-Avoidant/Disorganized might crave intimacy, but they're afraid of getting too close for fear of loss. They might have a hard time trusting people and tend to push others away. People who have experienced abuse, abandonment, or grief early in life might be more likely to initially adopt a Fearful-Avoidant attachment style. For adults, development is centered upon constantly perceived fear, they have difficulty trusting other people, and they can exhibit behavioral inconsistency to the extreme.[5]

If you're *Fearful-Avoidant/Disorganized*, you might have a hard time delegating because you don't trust anyone else to do the job. Or you could have a fear of success and therefore subconsciously sabotage new opportunities because you're afraid of the uncertainty that comes with success.

**Secure:** People who have a Secure attachment style tend to express their emotions appropriately, give and receive intimacy, and draw healthy boundaries. They're solution-focused. Their outlook on relationships and connection is generally positive. Not that people aren't without their faults and challenges, but this is the healthiest of the four styles.

If you're *Secure*, you confidently either win or walk away from new business because you know your worth, and you value your team members. You lead with compassion and are unafraid to be vulnerable or ask for help. You go out of your way to develop the potential in your people and demonstrate your trust in them through respectful, relevant delegation. You respect their boundaries and support their growth objectives.

In business, I've absolutely taken on less-than-ideal clients just to pay the bills and even discounted proposals without reducing the scope of work we were going to deliver. You, too? I've promised unrealistic deadlines because I wanted a client to praise our speed and competence. I've personally taken on execution work that wasn't an intelligent use of my time as the leader because I didn't trust that anyone else could do it as quickly or as perfectly as I would. If you're the founder of a service-based company, you know exactly what I'm talking about.

There's no judgment about which attachment style you have in this current phase of your life, or how you've repeated patterns in previous phases of your life. We are all products of the experiences that have blindsided us, as well as the choices we've made. The mind and body are geared toward survival. Your attachment style is a patterned response to things that have happened to you, so there should be zero blame, shame, or guilt for your identification in any season of your life. After all, humans are not compartmentalized beings; how you grew up significantly influences how you show up as an adult.

These styles of relational attachment are generalized categories, and we can exhibit tendencies from each throughout our lives. Aside from your own way of being in the world at particular phases of your life, pay attention to how those around you show up. Recognizing that your would-be client is dismissive-avoidant, for example, might give you a clue that she won't respond well to an excess of follow-up calls.

Meanwhile, your anxious-preoccupied employee might need continuous feedback that he's doing a good job.

> What impact would it have on you **not** to work toward a more secure style?

## Change as a Practice

Changing patterns that have been baked into your being is difficult and will not happen overnight. But once you know something new and foundational about yourself, you can never unknow it. The natural tendencies are either to distract yourself from the knowledge or take a step in the direction of evolution.

After identifying your primary attachment style—an act of self-awareness, by the way!—you're at a state where you might begin to unpack what's going on under the surface. From there, you can delve into its origination and work toward a more balanced approach to a few of the most important relationships in your life. The more conscious awareness you have, the more you can practice modifying your reactions, language, ability to pause and listen intently, level of empathy, and so on—before they derail your next deal or relationship.

> Identify your core or primary wounds.
>
> How might you have used leadership as a way to get your unmet needs met?
>
> What have you endured or imposed on others as a leader, as a result of your core wound?
>
> How has your trauma influenced your efficacy as a leader?

# 11

## An Awakening

FROM AN EXTRINSIC point of view, there are reflective points in our lives that force us into the light of waking up from the status quo of our existence. We know that real change is needed when we encounter our own resistance to others' objectivity or when difficulties pile up to the point where we believe we might never know the feeling of ease.

The universe has a way of offering us exactly what we need to see our entire world differently. The moment you lift your gaze and it hits you that none of your perceived experience is real—that's the ethos of awakening. Your priorities change. What you lend your attention to, the way you leverage your resources, and how you live on a day-to-day basis shift in a way that is dramatic and simultaneously subtle.

### Unemployable

In 2016, I was taking part in an MBA-style program offered by Goldman Sachs. As I worked on the growth plan for my marketing agency, I found myself wondering if anyone else felt like me: burned out and unhappy. During the program, a couple of coincidental discussions about merging or being acquired had surfaced with other agency owners. One was with another cohort member and the other was with the founder of the leading social impact agency. As I explored the pros and cons of each, a third option for acquisition presented itself.

I loved my team and the impact that our work had in the world—both for clients and within our local community where we volunteered as a group—but I was deeply unwell. Even though I never made the correlation while I was a CEO, I had relied on the business to fill the void that my core *mother wound* had created. I decided to explore the possibility of no longer running the cause marketing firm I had founded 14 years prior.

My awakening started the morning after signing the paperwork for the acquisition. I've never felt a deeper sense of panic, uncertainty, and despair in my life. I hadn't realized how entwined into my identity my title was. Childfree by choice, it felt as though I had sold off my teenage daughter. Post-acquisition felt like an apocalyptic scene from a movie, as if I was standing in the middle of a desolate city street, with smoke rising from the asphalt and deafening silence all around. I remember a visceral feeling of numbness. Everything I knew and loved and worked so hard to build had seemingly evaporated overnight. My ego was left pummeled again, and I was immobilized.

With no office door to walk through and no team around me, I felt lost and without direction. Instead of feeling elated upon reaching the societal holy grail of building a company from scratch, scaling, and then selling it, a vast hollowness pushed against all my internal edges. Knowing I would never work for the new firm, and under legal contract that I couldn't start another agency, or join one in a partnership capacity for three years, I told myself that a 36-year-old CEO was *unemployable*. It touched an unhealed place that has resided in me for a lifetime—being unemployable was equal to having *no value*, being *unwanted*, or *not mattering*.

It was an entirely invented narrative, but my psyche couldn't separate the story from reality. My CEO title was the only one I had known for well over a decade. I had built my world around my agency. And without a team of people—literally *without company*—I knew I would be alone. It felt like my sense of self was purchased in the process and now belonged to someone else. I felt rebranded without control. It took me months before I could even look at *their* website. The jackets and long-sleeved shirts embroidered with our logo made their way to the donation drop-off bins as part of a grieving process I never anticipated.

Over the course of those 14 years as a business leader, I never stopped to think about what was driving my entrepreneurial pursuits. I never once considered what kind of life I wanted to live, or if running the agency contributed to, or detracted from, my personal fulfillment. Was the reason I pushed so hard from such a young age to prove to myself and others that I was *valuable*? To prove to my mother that *I was enough*? Were the reasons behind *selling the company* also rooted in unhealed trauma—in that I didn't deserve to have the level of success I created for myself?

Self-doubt and shame seeped in, regardless of how many awards adorned our conference room shelves or how impressive our reputation was in the industry. The shame I felt five years prior about the failure of another venture had almost completely dissipated, but somehow the acquisition experience brought it right back, tenfold.

"Shame keeps worthiness away by convincing us that owning our stories will lead to people thinking less of us. Shame is all about fear. We're afraid that people won't like us if they know the truth about who we are, where we come from, what we believe, how much we're struggling, or believe it or not, how wonderful we are when soaring (sometimes it's just as hard to own our strengths as our struggles)," writes Brené Brown in *The Gifts of Imperfection*.[1] I wondered what other people would say. I thought about the various stories they'd invent about why I sold the firm. How would I answer their questions? I couldn't tell the truth. I didn't want anyone to find out that I was *just unhappy*. That didn't seem to be a valid enough reason to sell a company. So many other leaders were miserable in one way or another and *they* were able to power through. What did it say about me that I didn't want to keep going and growing? And what was I going to do now? The deluge of negative thoughts and anxiety was debilitating. Caring what other people thought caused so much suffering, and I was already depressed, barely able to see my way out of this perceptual quicksand.

## Dark Night of the Soul

Typically, any awakening caused by a significant life event changes the trajectory of your life because it has the potential to open you up to a different way of being and a complete shift in perspective. It took a solid six months before I found my footing. When I was finally able to breathe again and notice a bit of light in the distance, by some miracle, I decided to go *against* my first inclination to create the next thing. To immediately distract myself from all of these intense emotions, setting out to prove my worth and value to myself, the world (and my mother) again. Instead, I stepped inward. I started asking myself real questions about who I was, who I wanted to be, what I was deeply passionate about, how I wanted to live, whom I wanted to serve, and if there was a true purpose to this thing called *life*.

I had no idea how to answer these questions staring up at me from a sheet of paper. It was in that moment that I realized how terrifying loneliness and lack of belonging truly was. That theme repeated over the next few years, until I came to a stark realization just before my 40th birthday: we are so afraid to be alone in any capacity because it means that we actually have to encounter ourselves—and we will run from that at all costs.

> *"People will do anything, no matter how absurd, to avoid facing their own soul. One does not become enlightened by imagining figures of light, but by making the darkness conscious."*[2]

> **—Carl Jung**
> *PSYCHIATRIST AND PSYCHOANALYST*

One day after the acquisition was complete, I was cleaning out our offices. A friend and her new business partner popped in to say hello. They were opening a metaphysical shop across the street, and I was curious about what they would do and sell there. They asked me to help with their identity, website, and marketing collateral. The creative process of building their brand probably kept me from sinking into a deeper depressive state.

Over the next couple of years, I spent a lot of time there, attending nearly every workshop and class they offered. I met new friends who were intuitive, empathic, and powerfully gifted in ways I'd never encountered before. I felt like I was discovering a new sense of belonging. This world was simultaneously unfamiliar and also felt like a natural homecoming. The intuitive parts of myself that I had pushed away for so long were finally given permission to surface. The combination of new vocabulary and elevated consciousness training was exhilarating, and there was a knowing inside that I was finally ready to explore what *wholeness* meant for me.

As part of that journey, I began to release the physical weight that I had been carrying around for the length of time I owned my agency. I started to allow myself to be seen. Shortly thereafter, I engaged Anahita Moghaddam for mentorship in contemplative science and Buddhist psychology. I also hired Fereshta Ramsey as my shadow work coach for inner child healing. It was a commitment, and an investment in my well-being, and I had no idea that the combination of work would eventually lead me to emotional liberation.

## Leadership Lessons Learned

When we apply a holistic view to the trauma we experienced in our own lives, we can feel the example of wabi-sabi, the appreciation for imperfection, come to life. In *Why People Don't Heal and How They Can*, Caroline Myss writes, "We are not meant to stay wounded. We are supposed to move through our tragedies and challenges and to help each other move through the many painful episodes of our lives. By remaining stuck in the power of our wounds, we block our own transformation. We overlook the greater gifts inherent in our wounds—the strength to overcome them and the lessons that we are meant to receive through them. Wounds are the means through which we enter the hearts of other people. They are meant to teach us to become compassionate and wise."[3] My own psychological or emotional wounds, in fact, offered me the opportunity to discover the truth of who I am. What we learn and how we grow as a result of working through our trauma enables us to connect more deeply with ourselves and our plethora of relatives.

My experiences in business taught me that to lead an innovative and sustainable company, I had to find the courage to let go—to stop trying to control every aspect of our process, service delivery, and reputation. My natural ability to empathize with others enabled me to connect to most of my employees and clients easily, but my lack of self-worth allowed some of them to take advantage, which also highlighted my need to enact healthier boundaries. These are

a few examples of how anxious attachment can be cloaked as conscious leadership. And all of those experiences have shaped who I am
today. The ability to turn around previous perceptions of my leader-
self helped me see how and when I led from a wounded place. I saw
how that directly impacted the agency, even stunted its growth. From
there, I wanted to learn and understand how to change my mindset,
my feelings, and my behavior—and all of that began with taking a
responsible role in healing and integrating my childhood trauma.

It took me some time to figure out that is part of my purpose in
the world—to empower other leaders to heal so that they can lead
more effectively. Despite all of my first-hand experience with childhood trauma, traditional therapy, other healing modalities, personal
growth, and leadership development, I wouldn't come to recognize
that I was the right person for this role without being guided to it via
self-inquiry—and turning up the volume of my inner voice to listen to
the answers. I advocate to redefine *leadership* as *a healing journey*.

Along with the sale of my marketing firm came a three-year non-
compete agreement. I felt dejected; my options were so limited. It took
some time to figure out what I would do next because my amygdala was
on high alert, which blocked my ability to innovate. Then I applied a
series of questions to start to fill in the parts that felt cracked and made
me feel unsure about the future:

- *What am I most passionate about? What lights me up—inside and out?*
- *Where would my expertise be most valuable, and who would benefit
  most from my experiences?*
- *What kind of life do I want to live going forward?*

These questions initially led me to start an agency growth consultancy. The number of small to mid-sized creative, media, and technology
agencies in the United States alone was about 30,000 at the time. Most
agency owners feel like impostors and make decisions out of fear. Their
insecure leadership styles often lead to employee attrition. Most rely
predominantly on referrals—and for some it's even worse, as they rely
solely on request-for-proposals (RFPs), whereby work must be produced
as part of the response. Many founders want to sell their companies at
some point, or at minimum feel supported by a peer who has been in
their shoes.

I discovered that of the handful of consultants in this niche, very few had actually owned an agency outright, let alone sold it, and there were only one or two people in the industry who were not male. Since 2020, the landscape has become crowded as more agency owners have jumped ship to consult. I completely understand why. The money is great, you and your assistant are likely your only two employees, and you decide when, where, and with whom you'll work. There's no shortage of marketing and advertising leaders looking to scale their agencies and increase their profit margins.

For a few years, I enjoyed the work and the lifestyle that came along with it. As I helped agency after agency, it was rewarding to see their teams gel with clearer communication, healthier pipelines due to diversification and strong positioning, new accounts closed at higher rates, and systems and processes solidified to withstand the growth. Yet, if I'm honest, even this left me wondering if there was something I was missing, something that would feel like a more impactful deployment of my intuitive skills and life experience. I could feel myself inching closer, but I wasn't there yet.

## Discovering the Root

That inner knowing started gnawing at me. I saw progress among teams that tasted transparency for the first time. Better tools, systems, and processes allowed for improved communication, which resulted in less frustration, less duplication of effort, and—as a lagging indicator—higher profitability. Employees seemed happier overall, which led to better work and higher client satisfaction, more ideal referrals, and brand new business. Yet the empath in me could no longer ignore what I was feeling from nearly every agency leader who hired me: underlying personal fears stunted organizational growth. There was constant anxiety, overwhelm, reactionary behavior, and mental health struggles. Their leadership styles were the manifestation of their interiority, and they were searching for external support to fix whatever they perceived was wrong or lacking without ever looking inward.

Because I grew up with conflicting accounts between how my mother acted outside our home and how I was treated inside of it, I was an expert at observing behavior, verbal cues, body language, and the nuances of each. In business, my skills as an active and intent listener sharpened—to what was being said, what was purposefully not being said, and when and how to probe deeper. This was especially true with my consulting clients. Many believed they were doing a good job from a leadership standpoint, only to find out that their employees did not feel the same way because they were on the receiving end of the controlling or pleasing behavior and other unintegrated trauma responses.

The conditions in their own lives determined how they led. I realized that if I was going to help leaders transform their businesses, they needed to see what I was seeing, especially because they couldn't or didn't want to. It sounded more like therapy than anything else, and I knew it could be a hard sell. With its long-term stigma, no one likes to talk about mental health, emotional well-being, or the childhood trauma that's usually at the root of these things. My work shifted over time from business consulting for agencies to a hybrid approach that maintained the integrity of an inquisitive coaching container while separately providing conscious leadership consulting.

The ethos of my work in the world is now a direct reflection of the healing and guidance I needed as a leader. I provide one-on-one executive and group coaching—through a trauma-informed lens—to emerging and established leaders across industries. Together, we uncover their innate gifts, and how they can contribute in a world that needs them more now than ever. I also speak to audiences about the influence of childhood trauma on leadership style and how to unveil the high-conscious leader within.

## Full Circle

My first moments of self-awareness were the ones in which I recognized how unhappy I was within many areas of my life: my work, my marriage, and my body, among others. It was hard to fully experience joy, even when it seemed like I was having a good time with friends. I repeated unhealthy patterns throughout adulthood to gain the things that I needed, but never received, as a child. We all do this in some form or another; these underlying reasons are why we think, speak, and behave the way we do in interactions with others. By holding ourselves and feeling deeply rooted, we're able to give without expectation or attachment to any particular outcome. We're able to move through life with a fluidity that is grounded in a well of genuine security.

Speaking of fluidity, this is a gentle reminder that I am gender-fluid and use they/them and she/her pronouns interchangeably. As I learned how to guide myself through that uncertainty and through the unearthing of years of childhood trauma, I found myself emotionally exhausted, and yet heart-full. Once I recognized that I was actively loving my inner child, I developed a practice of letting that little one know that they were perfect exactly as they were. I told them that I would stand up for and keep them safe from here on out. No one would ever hurt her again. No one would ever keep her small. They mattered.

I promised that I would create a world in which we prioritized play. Together, we'd explore and create a reality rooted in love, compassion, and gratitude. We'd return to our essence, which is kind, generous, and full of invitational laughter. Sometimes when I go for a walk, I imagine in my mind that I'm holding their little hand in mine. The love I feel for her brings me a deep sense of peace. My chest feels expansive and filled with radiant light. Interactions like these bring tears to my eyes. And when the tears that fall are those of sadness, for all the years that I abandoned them and didn't keep them safe, I welcome those, too. I've never felt more alive or aligned in my life, actively healing myself and supporting others to do the same.

If there was a pivotal event in your life that caused you to see everything differently, what was it?

How has it changed you and/or your work in the world?

Next time you're out for a walk, hold the hand of the younger version of yourself. Sense what arises.

# 12

## Doing the Work

CLEARLY, IT TOOK me a long time to find this sense of alignment. The desire for control—whether internal or external—became a recurring theme in my life, from body dysmorphia to athleticism and good grades to the relationship with my mother. If you've ever been a straight-A student, excelled at a sport, lost a significant amount of weight, felt the need to micromanage others, or rose above someone else's belief that they could keep you down, then you know how addicting control can be. Diana Chapman, Jim Dethmer, and Kaley Klemp describe this as one of three core wants—approval, security, and control—"if I can't gain security through approval, I'll get it through control. If I can't earn your approval, then I'll try to control you and life."[1] We all know how well that plays out.

If you can separate the thought of control and what it feels like in your body, you'll begin to notice a very interesting phenomenon. The idea of control can cause an illusory feeling of freedom in the mind, like a dopamine hit. In the body though, control might feel tight, coiled, hardened, and forced—the opposite of liberation. I can attest that the ways in which I tried to control my weight, for example, led me to believe that the choices to eat, not eat, binge, or purge were mine. And they were, but they were based in fear of not being accepted (approval), fear of being unloved, and without a sense of belonging (security).

"The price for ignoring or distorting the body's messages is being unable to detect what is truly dangerous or harmful for you and, just as bad, what is safe or nourishing," says Bessel van der Kolk. "Self-regulation depends on having a friendly relationship with your body. Without it, you have to rely on external regulation—from medication, drugs like alcohol, constant reassurance, or compulsive compliance with the wishes of others."[2]

During our youngest years, we're wired to try to get the safety that we need.[3] And if suppressing an aspect of ourselves yields those results, it makes sense that we would continue to exercise that form of control. The suppression of anger meant that I had not given myself permission to express the full range of human emotion. And so it remained buried alive under years of accumulated silt in my body. When I was 38, I finally began to physically release some of the remaining emotional protection, in the form of shedding 40 pounds by eating healthy and exercising every day. I started with indoor circuit training for the first eight months, and then took up jogging and mountain biking on some of the trails near my house.

One day, my friend Ronan and I were talking about boxing after a recent conversation about our differing childhood experiences with being bullied. He is a martial arts instructor and trainer. My entire body tightened as he shared a video of his most recent workout on a water-filled aqua bag at a local gym. He asked if I had ever boxed, and I firmly said that I had not. Not only did I have zero interest, I couldn't even imagine putting boxing gloves on and hitting an inanimate object, let alone sparring with a partner. He felt compelled to lean in.

With the proper foundational footwork and training, he thought that boxing would be cathartic for me. Ronan's steady energy, big heart, and Irish brogue are quite the convincing combination. By the end of the conversation, I gave in. For the next few months, we would meet at the gym, focus on stance and shifting weight from leg to leg, positioning the gloves to protect my face, the fluidity of movement around the heavy bag, and, of course, sequences. Jab, jab, cross, left hook. When it became clear that the pandemic was going to keep us out of gyms, I ordered an 80-pound punching bag and hung it from one of the rafters in my detached garage. Several times a week, I would go out there after work, turn on my Heavy Bag playlist, and practice my footwork and sequences. It became a curious dance that was sometimes beautiful and fluid, and sometimes awkward and uncomfortable.

One particular afternoon, shortly into my regular routine and without any music in the background, I unleashed. That poor heavy bag never saw me coming. I jabbed multiple times in a row just to set it up for the strong right cross and left hook, then left cross and right hook. I wanted to hurt it. Many times, I found myself panting and hugging the thing. I purposefully pushed it circuitously around the garage just so I could wail on it every time it came toward me. I must have been in there for an hour or more. With a final arm-storm, I let it all out: the pent-up rage and anger was buried so deep—for not being seen or loved or accepted for who I was. For the unjust treatment. The screaming in my face. The hair pulling. The painful instruments on bare skin. The fingernails that drew blood. Open-palmed slaps, kicks, grabs, and body slams against walls. Every time I punched one out, another memory followed. If I wasn't in the midst of dealing with the surfacing of my own repression of anger, it would have felt like some sick game of whack-a-mole. I tried to keep up with the memories until I found myself oscillating between hitting and crying and punching and full-body exhaustion.

When it was all over, I collapsed on the floor of the garage, sobbing into my white leather boxing gloves. I tried to peel the thick Velcro off my wrists with my teeth, but I didn't have the strength. I just crouched there, forehead to the dusty floor, and let it all out. When I finally got up, the puddle was equal parts sweat, tears, and snot. I walked back into the house on shaky legs. Ironically, it was on those legs that I felt something shift in me, something I had never experienced before. The release of years of anger and resentment rising from the depths of my body, through my heart into my shoulders, arms, wrists, and fists. It felt like purging poison and a restoration of vitality.

It would be a full three years before I would punch a bag again. I couldn't step foot in there for a long time; she was in that garage. Luckily, I bought a house for myself so I had to move. But I needed time to accept the idea that taking out my repressed anger on a punching bag was a healthy way for me to discharge energy. Pushing down the anger I felt for being abused was a textbook survival mechanism; it represented the deep trauma that I couldn't look at for three decades.

As an adult, have you ever thought about the smaller, younger version of you—and all he/she/they experienced?

If the little version of you were sitting right by your side at this moment, what would they need to hear?

## What Is the Work?

When people talk about "doing the work," what they are actually referring to is anything but casual. It's the process of digging through layers of repressed emotion and otherwise breaking yourself open to let the light in.

Jeremy McAllister, an expert practitioner in the work of healing and integrating complex trauma, says, "After years of automated disconnection and internal judgment, integration is often felt as an awakening, a softening toward what was once perceived as an enemy, a protective hesitance becoming a grateful encompassing. It is felt most profoundly in the surprising arrival of ownership and empathy for Self." McAllister explains further, "It's the point at which we realize this 'part in exile' has been trying to get our attention, to elicit from us a response it never got from our caregivers. This gives us a chance to feel what it felt, to finally see it, to stop containing it as something evil and instead embrace it and feel with it."[4] If everything that needs to be integrated remains in the darkness, we can never feel the whole of who we truly are.

It's important to know that the process is also one that unfolds over time. It is not possible to heal years of wounding at once or even within a short period of time; learning first how to guide yourself through healing and the integration of past trauma takes commitment—literally, the commitment of a lifetime.

How you work on your past is entirely up to you, and it might also be helpful to see some kind of menu if you're unsure of where to begin. I have put together this one-of-a-kind resource (by no means an exhaustive list), categorized as Appetizers (Cerebral Resources), Sharing Plates (Therapeutic and Integrative Modalities), Entrees (Somatic Practices), and Dessert (Plant Medicine and Psychedelics—see note) to help you navigate the multitude of options available. Curiosity is a helpful

companion. Feel free to pause here and explore **MyHealingMenu.com,**
or keep reading and visit later.

> NOTE: *It's vitally important to be aware that the use of plant medi-*
> *cine and psychedelics should only be approached responsibly and with*
> *intention. Do your own research and seek guidance from trained pro-*
> *fessionals, as some can have significant effects on individuals' mental*
> *and physical well-being. For example, some of these are contraindi-*
> *cated for people taking monoamine oxidase-inhibiting harmala alka-*
> *loids (MAOIs) or selective serotonin reuptake inhibitors (SSRIs).*[5]

There are myriad avenues to explore in relation to healing and
integrating trauma. How, why, when, and what people gravitate
toward throughout their lifetime typically begins slowly and with the
more easily approachable options. Sometimes, as you're researching
more about a particular practice or modality that interests you, you
might discover something completely new and progress in that direction instead. This is precisely the intention of **MyHealingMenu.com.**

I've personally experienced 30 items from the menu over the last
25 years, and one of the more recent was from the Dessert section.
In October 2022, I engaged in my first Ayahuasca ceremony in the
Peruvian Amazon with two indigenous healers from the Shipibo tra-
dition. I like to think about plant medicine and psychedelics as the
dessert on the healing menu because you'll likely engage with these
less frequently than other modalities, and they can be the richest
of experiences. If you decide to, please take small bites and savor them
because the integration from these experiences might be the most
potent of all.

## The Journey of a Lifetime

I had resisted hallucinogens for so long because I enjoyed feeling in control. In case I felt paranoid, I wanted to be able to turn off the high. That
said, my experience with Ayahuasca was life-altering in the best ways
imaginable. I definitely do not recommend going from 0 to 60, having
never engaged with a psychedelic, and then sitting with Ayahuasca as
your first entry point, but I received a very clear message to share the
wisdom of this plant medicine through my experience.

At a small hotel in Tarapoto, Peru, our guides picked us up as part of a small participant group, and from the moment they arrived, the three facilitators began tracking each of us. They paid attention to our personalities, the language we used, how we held ourselves, whether or not we had engaged with the medicine before—and how much we purged during *vomitivo* the following morning. It is exactly what it sounds like. In our case, each person continuously drank several pints of cooled lemongrass tea until it was fully purged. This is done in an effort to cleanse the body for a ceremony later that evening.

When night fell in the middle of the Amazon rainforest, the facilitators and two Shipibo healers (one maestra and one maestro, cousins who had been taught by their grandfather) met us in the *maloka*, a large round structure on stilts with a conical ceiling and half-wood, half-screen walls. Behind a curtain there were three bathrooms and purposefully, no mirrors in sight. The facilitators and healers began to smoke *mapacho*, a pure form of native tobacco, to clear unwanted spirits or energies from the space. The ceremony started, and each person was given a specific dose of the dark, thick liquid to drink. After my brimming cupful—which I immediately questioned—I returned to my thin mattress. We were positioned two feet away from our neighbors on both sides, purge buckets situated directly next to us. Within 20 minutes, I began to feel my limbs getting heavy. My initial worry was that I might feel pinned down the entire time, but I just relaxed into feeling no pain in my body whatsoever. The very moment I created space for that relaxed energy, my visual world exploded into the most brilliant colors and four-dimensional shapes. There was movement to everything, in perfect tempo and rhythm; it was clear that everything was purposefully composed. The world was one big, beautiful, musical show. I couldn't quite believe that this performance was all for me. It was spectacular!

Within the first five minutes, I began dialoguing with the medicine inside my body. I was Kelly, having this supreme experience, and my conscious awareness was floating a foot above my right shoulder, observing everything I was experiencing. The best way I can describe it is that my consciousness was co-collaborating with the Ayahuasca vine. I told her how grateful I was for this experience already—I felt so revered and joyful. I also admitted that psychedelics were probably not for me, but I was going to receive as much as I could from this. I was all in and ready for what she wanted to show me.

With that, she began to respond to my first intention: *To be shown the content of my heart and my capacity for love.* I was taken upwards toward the sky, and as I soared higher, I could feel my heart swelling. I was giving and receiving love simultaneously, at a level I had never imagined possible. I was so curious how any emotion could feel this expansive until I hovered in front of the farthest edge of the blue sky and watched it start to dissipate in front of me. Visually, the pixel-like wall began to erode and fade away. Behind it, the cosmos exposed: the entire universe, with stars, planets, and other galaxies in the distance as far as I could see. I asked, "What is this that you're showing me?" She replied, "This is your heart. Your heart is as big as the universe." I kept repeating, "That big? It's that big?" The feeling in my chest, as I encountered the truth of what I had likely known but never wholeheartedly believed, brought a newfound acceptance of who I was. Who I am. Who I have always been. I took some time to receive this truth, to let it into my consciousness. Those moments were the fullest my heart has ever felt. I basked in the ecstatic feeling, as though the sun was warming my face and love was the only thing I had ever known.

In contrast to the saturated colors and visual depiction of the size of my heart, there was a transition to some gray matter; I felt like I was in a tank of water filled with giant cotton balls. It was a strange sensory experience but not frightening. I inquired and I came to find that I was inside my stepmom's brain. After I discovered why I was there and was given specific information to share with her about her parents, I landed in a sterile, white room. I was shown a rolling cart with intravenous drip bags hanging, about a dozen bags on a single bar. Mama Aya asked how many I would take, but I didn't understand. I assumed it was saline because the liquid was clear. She explained that each bag contained the tears of humans who had experienced terrible things, from war to wrongful imprisonment to sexual violence, physical abuse, and so on. It was a buffet of big "T" trauma, and I was asked if I would take on any of this collective pain. I tried to wrap my head around the scenario for a moment, and then I agreed to have 7 of the 12 bags injected into my arm. That felt like the amount I had the capacity to transmute on behalf of humans who could not integrate these traumatic experiences on their own.

As the scene started to pan away, I wondered, "Wait, what now?" She said to me, "This is also the capacity of your heart. You agreed to take other people's pain because you know how to help them heal. You're selfless, and yet you're wise enough not to take every bag; you know how to sustain yourself." Even now, I marvel at the creative construction of that vignette and how sensational it was at responding to my intention.

During the remainder of the hallucinogenic trip, I was shown how so many of my young decisions and behaviors were directed by my intuition. Even though I couldn't understand when I was younger, I had a deep knowing about how to ensure life—including protecting myself from my mother. I was also shown the importance of keeping my mind and body clean now, as a channel for *metacognition*, or *spiritual intelligence*.[6] The directive from the medicine was: no alcohol, no smoking (cannabis or tobacco), no caffeine, no meat (animal or bird), and no pornography (where the minds of men have been poisoned by disrespect or aggression toward others). It felt clear and in alignment. Agreeing to this lifestyle for the benefit of myself and other beings felt as easy as breathing.

When it was Maestra Tanya's time to sing directly to me, she took a seat two feet away. I sat cross legged on the edge of my mat, bucket in hand as she started to sing. To pull out the purge, *icaros* are medicinal songs that "can be used to heal a wide range of illnesses . . . to call helper-spirits, to recover lost souls, to travel through various cosmological-spiritual realms, and to increase, decrease, and modulate the visual effects of psychoactive plant-medicines, among many other uses."[7] The healers drink the medicine, too, to connect with the plant medicine inside of our bodies. While I couldn't understand the Shipibo words being sung, the sentiment and emotion was clear, much like listening to an Italian opera if you don't speak Italian. Tanya's song morphed from swooning to sadness to lullaby over the course of about half an hour. I had never felt as cared for by someone I had never known before. My eyes were closed the entire time, and it was as if we were the only two people in the *maloka*, though there were 14 other humans in close proximity, smoking, singing, wailing, sniffling, and purging. As she sang, Tanya's tone pulled me down, and I bowed my head in sorrow. I felt worthless, hopeless, and alone—emotions that often arose during childhood, but ones that I never allowed myself to feel fully. And now they were making me ill so that I could become well.

As I began to feel nauseous, I wondered if this was one of the primary reasons I had come to this place. I purged once. I consented verbally to the medicine: "This is why I'm here." With that, Tanya's song pulled me lower and the felt sense of my own body began to transform into a sickly, rat-like creature. I was an entity that no one cared about. It didn't matter whether I lived, suffered, or died. I held no value, my existence meant nothing, and I was starting to die. The *maestra* brought me to the very place I subconsciously feared as a kid. The mixture of my own vomit and the foul odor of decomposition hit me in the face. All of a sudden, the bottom of my bucket dropped out, and my dying body fell through the plastic pail onto the damp floor of a cold, dark basement like a small, wet mop thrown onto concrete. There was no light, but I could make out some basic laboratory equipment—a Bunsen burner, some beakers, and a few test tubes in a stand. It's hard to believe, but none of the experiences up to this point frightened me; they just were, and I continued to consent. Then the four concrete walls of the basement fell away simultaneously, and all that was left was nothingness. I realized this is how I would die, my body decomposing while my mind was still conscious. No warmth, no love, no connection, just alone, rotting and not mattering to anyone or anything. The combination of feeling untethered in the dark vastness and having no value was enough to make me purge a concentrated amount from the depths of my guts. Each drop of bile was collected in a test tube, and when it was full, I was shown that these were the last ounces of poison from my mother. It was clear to the plant that I had done much healing work on my own, but this particular sludge was inaccessible to me prior to this moment. The collected specimen served as a form of confirmation that something deep was dimming my light and limiting my access to love, play, and joy—the very things I was shown at the onset of my journey. I finally understood that my value is inherent in my being and that no external entity could ever determine my worth.

Tanya sprayed a fine mist of *Colonia de Ruda* from her mouth—a shamanic ritual cologne. I lay on the mat, completely exhausted. Soon after, one of the facilitators came over to ask if I felt well enough to sit at the edge of my mat for Maestro Gabriel; I was the last person to receive an *icaro* from him that evening. The focus of his song touched upon the usage of my voice for meaningful awakening in the world.

While I didn't purge like I did before, Gabriel's song was energetically trying to unhinge and break my jaw. His *icaro* also sealed an ancient wound where my throat was cut during my first incarnation—hence the voicelessness. When all was done, I laid down again for several hours, tossing and turning, until I saw the black sky begin to turn navy. When it became light enough to leave, my friend and I returned to our rooms after one of the most intense evenings of our lives.

My body would fully recover in about a week, but my mind was completely rewired as I began to process what I had just seen, learned, and experienced in that *maloka*. I would never be the same version of me that existed prior to that ceremony—a pivotal before-and-after moment in my life.

About a month after Peru, I began microdosing psilocybin with the intention to help increase awareness, enhance creativity, recall distant memories, and continue to explore oneness with the natural world. At 1/20 of a typical dose of magic mushrooms, the impacts are incredibly subtle and without any of the hallucinatory effects like I had in the Amazon with Ayahuasca. Yet even in its subtlety, I could tell that something was shifting within me, as if it was happening in the background while I was playing in the foreground. I noticed natural elements more easily and was enchanted by them. I felt energized by pursuits that were much greater than me. I was moved by kindness and magnetized to helping people move through their emotions.

## How Do I Know the Work Is Working?

As we explored in the *Spiral of Healing*, the path is anything but linear. From the resources, modalities, practices, and psychedelics listed on **MyHealingMenu.com**, you have a starting point at the very least.

> "A healed life is always a work in progress, not a life devoid of all suffering, but a life lived fully, deeply and authentically, compassionately engaged with the world."[8]

**—Miriam Greenspan**
*HEALING THROUGH THE DARK EMOTIONS*

Pain is usually our gateway into seeking resources because we feel as if we don't know where else to turn. Either that or life provides us with a wake-up call we cannot ignore. Recognizing progress when working to heal from childhood trauma can be a complex process. When something is nonlinear, it involves a lot of ups and downs. Nonetheless, you'll know that the work is working when you begin to notice more peace than fear as you practice letting go, recall and remember your worth, spend time alone and find yourself loving it, trust yourself to make decisions without external input, and embrace stability, especially if chaos has been your comfort zone. Beyond these, there are several other signs that might indicate evolution:

- **Reduced intensity of emotional reactions:** You might notice that situations, thoughts, or feelings that used to activate strong emotional responses in you now have a less intense effect and/or you might discover the ability to pause before reacting to situations or people that used to activate you.
- **Improved relationships:** You might find that your relationships with others improve because you're developing better communication skills or because you're better able to establish boundaries. You might also find yourself attracted to healthier relationships and naturally removing yourself from those that no longer align.
- **Better self-understanding:** Healing often involves gaining a deeper understanding of yourself. You might begin to recognize patterns in your behavior that you didn't see before, or understand the sources of certain feelings or reactions.
- **Less avoidant behavior:** Many people with trauma develop strategies to avoid activating situations or feelings. As you heal, you might find that you're less reliant on these avoidance strategies and more able to confront challenging situations directly.
- **Reduced physical symptoms:** Trauma can manifest in the form of chronic pain, inflammation, stomach problems, headaches, or other physical symptoms. As you process your trauma, you might find that these symptoms start to decrease or dissipate altogether, but sometimes that occurs after they worsen.

- **Increased ability to experience positive emotions:** If trauma has made it difficult for you to feel happiness, joy, or satisfaction, healing might allow you to regain the ability to experience these positive emotions.
- **Improved self-care:** You might notice that you're taking better care of yourself physically—eating healthier, exercising more, getting better sleep, and spending more time in nature.

## Why Is Integration So Important?

One of the most impactful yet often overlooked methods of integration is *rest*. In our society, we tend to devalue ideas and actions that seem simplistic, so we automatically discount them. As we work through our thoughts and feelings, correlating those to prior memories, it can feel emotionally or energetically depleting. When we rest our bodies, we have the opportunity to absorb, digest, and incorporate the new information we've been given during the healing process—whether it is something we read, listened to, talked through, experienced, or released somatically.

Throughout my own healing journey, I've recognized the need to slow down, take a step back, and make space for the integration of these new resources. I tended to move from one thing to the next as a business owner—and I still do more often than I'd care to admit. The constant stimulation, whether mental or physical, keeps me busy and distracted from the periods of rest that I know are imperative for my health and well-being.

The practice of *intentional resting*—not waiting until we're dead tired, but either scheduling rest as part of each day, or choosing rest over anything else—also offers a more frequent ability to pause. As you learn to integrate your past experiences, you'll slowly begin to recognize your own reactionary mechanisms and incorporate routines of self-care that enable you to self-sustain over time.[9]

The work of healing our history is not easy. Moments of profound realization are usually mixed with emotional releases like crying, laughter, anger, sadness, or grief, as well as physical pain, aching, or purging. Integrating this new information we learn about ourselves throughout the process of healing is essential. Aside from rest and stillness, other forms of integration include walking in nature, journaling, meditation, soaking, silent or other retreats, talking with a trauma-informed practitioner, energy work, and others.

EMDR-certified therapist Monica Mouer explains, "Psychological integration is a coming together of the parts of an individual. It speaks to the idea of unburdening and healing wounded parts of the self in order to allow your true identity to become fully engaged in life and relationships. To integrate is to become whole."[10]

During the first week of integration, post-Ayahuasca but still in Peru, I sat down with my journal:

Dear Mom,

I have the utmost compassion for the conditions in your life that have led you to where you now exist. When I was shown writing you a letter in my journey, I questioned why because I've tried that before. Now, I understand. Mom, I love you. I don't know if I've ever written those words. I'll never know how you feel when no one is around, but I hope you feel comfort and peace, knowing that if I could, I would purge your pain for you. My heart is pure and my love is infinite. And, if part of my lesson in this life is to speak up, hear me when I say how much I love you—for giving me life and for knowing what I needed by walking away.

Love,

Kelly

# PART

# IV

# True Strength

"If you're not uncomfortable in your work as a leader, it's almost certain you're not reaching your potential as a leader."[1]

—Seth Godin
*AUTHOR, ENTREPRENEUR, AND TEACHER*

VULNERABILITY IS THE courage to lean into the discomfort of being true to yourself, and that requires a different kind of strength than the one we've all been taught to associate with leadership. By replacing the impossible idea that you have to keep your professional and personal selves split, and remain emotionally distant from colleagues, we can begin to see the clear advantages of emotional exposure: expansion of consciousness and a sense of belonging for ourselves and approachability and connection with others.

It takes courage to admit that you don't have all the answers, let alone a full-blown solution to a particular challenge. Beyond that, it takes bravery to share any personal experiences, core wounds, failures, or missteps, no matter when they occurred in your life. While low-conscious leaders continue to view vulnerability as a form of weakness or submission, nothing could be further from the truth. We've all been lied to—for centuries; the key to human connection is comfort with vulnerability.

Embodying the practice on a daily basis is also part of doing the work. And as leaders, we need to be mindful of when, how, and how often we share parts of ourselves with others. If we overshare out of a trauma response, we might cause unnecessary worry in those whom we lead. If we don't share enough, we could lose connection. It's a mindful dance of knowing ourselves and our audience. We need to learn what's appropriate and relevant to share, consider whether or not we might activate others, and actively choose what's right for everyone given all the information we have in that moment.

We will get it wrong sometimes. So part of the ongoing practice is also to expect and accept that fact. To recognize that you are not responsible for the emotional reactions of others, not to ruminate and shame ourselves for missteps, and to learn how to share truths and parts of ourselves in ways that help, heal, invite, or inspire others.

What you do with all of these truths about vulnerability is very much up to you. What you might choose to share, with whom, and when are very personal decisions. Just like other aspects of healing, there is no right or wrong way to be vulnerable.

# 13

## Fundamental #2: Embodying Vulnerability

FROM HEALING OUR traumatic experiences—and being able to distinguish between reality and our false narratives—the ability to be vulnerable is born. As opposed to historical association with weakness, vulnerability makes leaders more approachable, more trustworthy, and more human to those they lead. It also brings people together in times of crisis, transition, or transformation.

If taking radical responsibility for one's own emotions and being willing to be authentically vulnerable are proven to be powerful leadership tools, how did we veer so far off course?

### A History Lesson

The concept of vulnerability has a long and complex history, particularly in terms of how it's been understood and valued. Its interpretation has evolved significantly over time, shaped by changing societal values, philosophies, and ideologies. Vulnerability was often seen as a weakness across many societies, and this perception was informed by a wide array of cultural, social, and even biological factors. Individuals who showed signs of vulnerability were perceived as less capable of contributing to the group's survival or even as a potential burden, risk, or threat to survival. Thus, vulnerability—susceptibility to harm or damage—was seen as a trait that might endanger the individual and their entire community, and must therefore be avoided.

Many societies place great value on traits such as physical strength, courage, and self-sufficiency, often considered the antithesis of vulnerability. These traits have long been associated with survival, prosperity, and power, particularly in eras when life was a daily struggle against the harsh realities of nature, conflict, and disease.

The stigma associated with vulnerability is entrenched in many philosophical, religious, and social norms. Many religions valorize figures who demonstrated strength in the face of adversity. That's why expressing emotions, admitting mistakes, or seeking help has been viewed as a sign of weakness for so long.

In recent decades, the perception of vulnerability has undergone a significant shift, particularly in the realms of psychology, leadership, and interpersonal relationships. In leadership, the traditional model often emphasized authority, decisiveness, and emotional stoicism; however, contemporary leadership theories increasingly value emotional intelligence, empathy, and authenticity, all of which involve a high degree of vulnerability. Leaders who embrace vulnerability are more likely to foster trust, create safe spaces for dialogue and innovation, and build strong, resilient teams. A variety of factors contributed to this shift:

- **Greater awareness and acceptance of mental health:** As more people talk openly about being in therapy or their mental health, we develop a better understanding of the importance of emotional vulnerability as a society. It is now widely understood that acknowledging feelings and seeking help when necessary are not signs of weakness, but require courage and are crucial for maintaining mental well-being.
- **Changing paradigms:** Command and control have given way to more collaborative, empathetic approaches to leadership. Increasingly, leaders are expected to be emotionally intelligent, to build connections with their teams, and to create psychologically safe environments where people can express their thoughts and feelings. Being vulnerable is now seen as a crucial component of modern leadership.

- **Research:** Psychologists and researchers have demonstrated the value of emotional intelligence and vulnerability in promoting personal growth, building trust, and fostering strong relationships.
- **Movements and media influence:** Social movements advocating for greater recognition of diversity, equity, inclusion, belonging, and accessibility emphasize the importance of vulnerability in acknowledging white privilege, understanding the experiences of others, and fostering change. Social and traditional media have also played a role, with many public figures sharing their own experiences and challenging traditional notions of strength and weakness.

For leaders, embodying vulnerability also gives permission for others to show up more authentically within organizations. It creates more human connection, which in turn creates more collaboration and creative risk-taking. The rise of team-oriented work environments has highlighted the importance of vulnerability in fostering effective team dynamics. Despite this shift, the association of vulnerability with weakness hasn't completely disappeared, but the increasing recognition of vulnerability as a leadership strength represents a significant change in our understanding of this complex human trait.

## Time to Come Clean

When I needed to tell my team that I wanted to sell the agency, I was frozen with fear about when to share the news, what to say, how they might react, who would think differently of me, or worse. I wanted to be honest that I felt like I was meant for more than running a digital agency, but I felt shame for being so willing to sell the company that we all cared about. This was my baby, birthed 14 years earlier with a single Mac laptop and $250 in my checking account. It wasn't just the company I had mixed feelings about selling and entrusting to someone else, it was the team itself, the intellectual property, the reputation we had all worked so hard to achieve, and our clients—some of whom had been with us for over a decade.

The day arrived. I had always been honest with my team, so I took a deep breath to calm my nerves, said that I had some big news to share, and proceeded to tell them about the three different conversations I recently had regarding selling the firm. I didn't want anyone to panic, but I was shaking a bit myself. I let them know that I had not made a decision as to which company would acquire us, and that I would share all three company names with them. No matter what, I promised to make sure that each of them landed on solid ground. They would have the option of joining the new company, or, if they decided to work elsewhere, I would personally help them with their search. I tried to create a space where any question could be asked, but my team needed to process the gravity of the news I had delivered. I wondered if I had made a mistake. There are many ways that the news could have been conveyed, but despite my fear, this level of transparency so early in the process felt aligned with the culture we had built together. It felt right in my body, despite my heightened anxiety.

Just then, our server administrator and lead solutions architect, Kevin, spoke up. "You should choose the option that works best for you. I think I can speak for everyone when I say that you've taken really good care of us, and we'll all be fine. We're all young and we'll figure it out. Do what you need to do to be happy." The majority of the team nodded in agreement. Gaby chimed in, "Yeah, what Kevin said." Five years later I asked Kevin to share his recollection of the disclosure that day. After taking some time to reflect, he wrote:

> One day, Kelly got everybody together in the office for a group meeting. She expressed interest in selling the company after receiving a few offers, and she wanted everyone's input. She wanted to make sure everyone felt heard, and that in some way, it was as much our decision together as it was hers; she truly valued the opinions of her people. I respected this so much, yet it sort of bewildered me—that she'd leave the future of her own career up to her team. Up to this point, I not only saw Kelly as a leader and mentor, but as a friend. In my opinion, the mere concept that she'd even considered selling the company, more or less part of her life's work at that point, indicated that she was, at least spiritually, ready to move on to her next chapter. To linger for

the benefit of others might not necessarily do her any good, and a determined leader like Kelly deserves nothing less than something worthy of her full commitment, attention, and soul. I've spent a lot of time reflecting on this moment: how someone as determined to excel and grow as Kelly is would potentially sacrifice the sale of her firm to see those around her grow and prosper. I had never doubted her resolve as a conscientious leader up to this moment, and that meeting has always stood out to me as a reflection of her character. Though the decision to sell, which I fully backed the moment I heard it, temporarily put me out of a job, I couldn't be more pleased to have followed Kelly as a leader then—and an entrepreneur in the years since.[1]

I tried so hard not to shed a tear while we were all sitting in that room, but a few inevitably fell. I was so moved by the support from these incredible humans in my moment of uncertainty, even though it meant that their employment would change one way or another. I'm positive that they must have experienced some instantaneous anxiety themselves, yet they were gracious, grateful, and made me realize that this was the ultimate in relational reciprocity. That moment was a gift. It is one of many specific examples of what can happen when a company's culture centers on collaboration, empathy, transparency, respect, and trust.

## Healthy Vulnerability

The embodiment of vulnerability—to be a consistent, living expression of what healthy vulnerability looks like—includes being transparent with teams and fostering environments that are psychologically safe. Knowing the difference between honesty and emotional outpouring is a practice. Within a workplace environment, the ability to discern what, when, how, and with whom to share is paramount; go too far and some of your colleagues or employees might take on the emotional burden of worrying about you. When sharing parts of yourself or asking for help when you need it, it's important also to be cognizant of creating sacred space, allowing others to do the same, and not confusing your willingness to be vulnerable with the opportunity to unload. I used to think of this discernment as a skill, but my mind was changed after reading a piece in the *Harvard Business Review* by Janice Omadeke. She says, "It's easy to think of vulnerability as a skill, but when we do, we distort the value of being vulnerable in the first place. The point of being vulnerable is sharing the authentic parts of yourself that you may have otherwise chosen to hide or keep private. Doing so is a personal choice—rather than a skill—that we weigh every day. It requires the self-awareness to ask, Will being honest in this moment serve me? Will it serve others?"[2]

If vulnerability feels out of reach, or if you're worried that you'll say the wrong thing, share too much, or feel mortified after the fact, there's good news. As a practice, embodying vulnerability is less about divulging big personal news and more about the micro-sharing of personal impact as the leader—for the benefit of others.

## The Mother Wound

Sharing with you that I led my agency from a subconscious core fear of abandonment feels vulnerable, even now. For me, the unhealed mother wound was as deep and far reaching as it could get, and was absolutely the basis for the impostor syndrome I felt from time to time throughout my career, particularly in leadership roles.

While the mother wound is most often associated with daughters, it is possible for any child to be impacted by a mother who suffers from alcoholism, drug addiction, or mental health conditions, whether diagnosed or not, treated or not. This lack of mothering reduces self-esteem, feelings of self-worth, and one's sense of mattering. Deeply rooted feelings about the need for perfection and control are most often associated with this type of psychological wounding, so it's easy to see how this could translate into impostor syndrome for some leaders.[3] In the next chapter, where I unpack impostor syndrome in-depth from multiple perspectives, you'll also see how being a member of the LGBTQIA+ community makes this a double whammy.

Though it has been easy to fall into, there is also a reality in which you can be in the process of unlearning and expanding at the same time you're guiding others. In fact, any other option is impossible because healing is never-ending. Personally, I wouldn't trust anyone who believes they have everything figured out and therefore have no further growing or learning left to do. Many unconscious leaders operate each day from this place, and these are the very people we distrust the most. They are so afraid of failing, or being perceived as a failure, that their egos construct a brilliant mechanism whereby they convince themselves that they are not impostors. They are self-proclaimed experts, seemingly wealthy and happy.

## The Social Construct of Failure

Consumerism runs on comparison. We see this play into our foundational fears in the advertising that interrupts our YouTube videos and Instagram feeds. The thing that people are most afraid of, especially in the United States, is that people will find out that they are either poor or sad; both are interpreted as failure. This is why low-conscious leaders disbelieve that telling the truth about human struggles with mental health, finances, or anything else could be beneficial.

High-conscious leaders are willing to let their humanity show. At some point during our healing journey, the attachment or association between vulnerability and failure diminishes. I talk openly about the trauma I experienced and the healing modalities with which I have engaged, like Ayahuasca, because I see the reactions that people have. They want to know much more. They share their stories, meaningful connections are made, and they transfer that impact to others. Society is ready for an approach to leadership that rails against the status quo. Instead of stoic and fearless, we are becoming bolder in the conscious approach to how we lead.

Embodying vulnerability—not just sharing something personal at a holiday work party—is fundamental to developing trust with those within your organization. When you come to realize that you are not at battle and you let the armor fall, the people who follow you will see you in a different light. They will better understand who you are and what it is that you stand for. They will rally around your cause and their peers. You will effectively set a new tone for the kind of environment that allows everyone simply to be human. And the guaranteed phenomenon is that your employees will become more trusting, more loyal, and more productive—all as a result of your vulnerability. See, when we talk about human nature, this is what we mean. We were built to thrive in community, so when a leader is trustworthy, those they lead change the way they show up as well. They let their guards down, too. A greater sense of comradery is felt. This is not a theory. I'm speaking from first-hand experience as a leader and subsequently as a coach to leaders and their employees. Vulnerability changes everything.

What's one thing you'd like to share openly with those you lead, but fear has held you back?

# 14

## Failure's Great Gift

A few years into running my marketing agency, I had the idea to launch a holistic health platform. I saw a gap in the market and I love the strategic thinking and creativity that's required for multifaceted business models. The idea was to help wellness practitioners market themselves more effectively, pair natural products providers with their target consumers—and schools and certification programs with their ideal students—and provide people interested in alternative medicine and complementary healing modalities with educational content and resources.

It was just before the 2008 recession when I started the Holistic Option. My timing has historically been this impeccable. It's almost like each time I launch something new, I purposefully wait for the full count—just like back in those softball days when it was my turn at bat. The business model itself was nicely diversified and included recurring monthly subscription fees for practitioners to be on the national, web-based directory (vetted by a top advisory board), advertising revenue from podcast sponsors and website banner ads, and ticket sales from in-person, educational events. I bootstrapped a good portion, took out a personal loan, and the remainder of the start-up funding came from seed money from friends, family, and colleagues who believed in me, the concept, and the larger vision in the world.

To say that there was a lot of pressure on my shoulders is a vast understatement. I was a young entrepreneur, now starting a second venture before the first one had its legs under it. It was underfunded because access to capital is near impossible for young founders, especially queer, female-presenting ones. The platform itself cost a quarter of a million dollars to build, there was a PR firm on retainer, a salesperson employed on base salary plus commission, and I was handling everything else. Working hard to ensure that everyone who invested was going to benefit financially was a next-level feeling of responsibility—all while running a bustling digital marketing agency. Plus, I had moved away from friends and family to Brooklyn, New York, while in a relationship that I knew wouldn't last, and I was feeling increasingly uncomfortable in my own physical body. My nervous system didn't stand a chance.

Did the venture succeed? Of course not. The seven shareholders took a loss when I had to offload the company three years later for no monetary gain other than to keep the podcast going and to roll the practitioners into a competitor's wellness platform. It landed me in personal debt of over $110,000 well before the age of 30.

I'm grateful for its so-called failure. I say so-called because while the traditional definition of financial failure might be obvious, I learned more from that experience than some business owners will come to know in their entire careers. Many of the connections I made during those three years are still strong today. I was even podcasting back when it was considered a fad and had the opportunity to host the number one show on iTunes (now Apple Podcasts) in the Health category for an entire year. I interviewed Deepak Chopra's daughter Mallika, actress and holistic mom Mayim Bialik, and best-selling author Dr. Bernie Siegel, to name a few.

If you consider that the entire experience with the Holistic Option cost me the equivalent of an MBA from Harvard, it was actually quite the bargain. I learned a tremendous amount about natural health, the importance of market research, the level to which people believed in me, and the importance of focus. I let that slip from my digital agency. Splitting my time, energy, and financial resources between two companies was not sustainable at that time in my life. My agency was years away from running without me in the day-to-day operations, and the vision I had for the Holistic Option was premature for the market in 2007, regardless of the impending recession.

One of the hallmarks of grounded leadership is recognizing all of the ways in which you've benefitted, grown, and learned invaluable lessons from experiences that historically have been associated with shame and guilt. Of course, that wasn't always the case for me. Stories about failure are far more interesting now than stories of success, as defined purely from a profit-to-shareholders, perspective. The plethora of lessons learned has since informed the start of new ventures that required very little capital and were quickly profitable. Had it not been for that epic failure, I would not have had the confidence or acumen to build again and again. I wear that epic failure as a badge of honor now—and not as a pro-resilience campaign.

As leaders, we tend to have tunnel vision and power through without listening to our intuition or considering where we might have blind spots. In retrospect, the business had to fail. I had to fail to take another step on the path toward self-discovery. I had to learn that creating a visionary business at the beginning of a recession with too little funding and even less market demand was more about *proving myself valuable* again than it was about creating something with consciousness, integrity, and sustainability in mind.

After the fire sale that was the Holistic Option, I turned my attention and focus back to my agency. In doing so, I felt a deep sense of shame. I felt as if *I was a failure*, not a *person who had failed at a start-up*. It was difficult to reacclimate because a shameful person cannot lead in any meaningful way. To lead others, we must first be able to lead ourselves, and I wasn't there yet—not by a long shot.

Have you ever failed at something big—only to realize the myriad positive impacts it had on your life?

## Impostor Syndrome

Most of us suppress unwanted emotions because facing them is too painful. Some numb with food, alcohol, drugs, sex, or retail therapy. Some retreat into the socially acceptable distraction of long work hours and the hustle culture. And those of us whom society has deemed "successful" don't feel any closer to free just because we've achieved the so-called American Dream. In fact, I'd argue that outward success without inner peace only ensures suffering. We remain small, caged by our own self-protection and emotional suppression, and really quite unhappy. This is the shared experience that so many of us have, especially as organizational leaders.

All of this suppression leads to *impostor syndrome* for many leaders—a so-called phenomenon where we feel like a phony, believe that we are incompetent from an intellectual standpoint, and that when we are successful, we chalk it up to luck or good fortune because we don't inherently believe in ourselves.[1] We worry that we'll be found out at any moment, as if we're a fraud within whatever role we hold. Impacting about 70% of us at some point in our careers, this feeling is pervasive for some people and can become debilitating.[2] For others, it can fade over the course of our careers. Early research initially theorized (and found) that women disproportionately report having experienced impostor syndrome, but newer research says that either men and women experience impostor syndrome equally, or men experience higher levels of anxiety particularly after receiving negative feedback and/or when they are held accountable to a higher authority.[3] My theory on the latter has to do with inflated confidence and ego due to our patriarchal society.

Before we continue, it does feel important to note a few things. First, several studies over the years have found that women *suffer* from impostor syndrome more than men, and I don't want to gloss over those so-called findings. Instead, I'd like to highlight an undeniable truth: the concept of impostor syndrome—coined initially as *impostor phenomenon* (IP) in 1978 by psychologists Pauline Rose Clance and Suzanne Imes[4]—"excluded the effects of systemic racism, classism, xenophobia, and other biases, took a fairly universal feeling of discomfort, second-guessing, and mild anxiety in the workplace and pathologized it, especially for women."[5] In digging deeper, I learned from researcher writers Ruchika Tulshyan and Jodi-Ann Burey that participants in that study were homogenous, and as a result of the psychologists' findings, the impact on women of color, as well as other genders, socioeconomic classes, and professions has been detrimental, because it puts the onus on the individual to deal with their mental affliction, as opposed to calling out the fact that the workplace was designed from the onset as a place where *we don't belong*. As Tulshyan and Burey encapsulate, "Fix bias, not women . . . impostor syndrome directs our view toward fixing women at work instead of fixing the places where women work." I agree wholeheartedly that it's not about repairing the deficits of individuals, but creating conscious work environments "where diversity of racial, ethnic, and gender identities is viewed just as professional as the current model," that is, "Eurocentric, masculine, and heteronormative,"[6] or the cis/het/white male model.

Second, as of the publication of this book, there has been zero research done on how leaders outside of the gender binary of male and female experience impostor syndrome. As a gender-fluid leader, I am particularly interested in this. The sole exception I found is the bachelor's degree capstone project of Kira C. Rideout from 2021, which sought to answer this question: "Are people who are a part of the LGBTQ+ community more likely to experience impostor syndrome than people who are not a part of the LGBTQ+ community?" While Rideout's research found a significantly higher rate of impostor syndrome in those who identify as part of the LGBTQ+ community, gender identity and sexual identity are not synonymous. We assume that if someone identifies as agender, bigender, gender-fluid, genderqueer, gender-nonconforming, or nonbinary, they are also likely to identify as part of the LGBTQ+ community, but that is not the case. Rideout concluded that "people who already feel like they are not a part of society are more likely to struggle with impostor syndrome. Most people do not want to feel isolated from their community and individuals who have impostor syndrome feel as if they are deceiving those around them."[7]

People of color tend to be especially vulnerable to impostor anxiety due to chronically high levels of stress in the workplace. Writer Alexandra Owens adds, "Coupled with a lack of representation and discrimination, the effects of imposter syndrome can feel nearly insurmountable [for minority groups]. After all, how do you wrestle with your own self-doubt when society is also telling you that you don't belong?"[8] Not surprising in an oppressive culture. What is surprising to me, though, is that we still accept that the likely causes of impostor syndrome are the "personality traits" of *perfectionism* and *anxiety* as well as a *family background* of "high-achievement" or "low support and high-conflict."

It seems to me that *family background* speaks more to psychological wounding, but we certainly can't call it trauma! My contention is that we move past language that makes us feel comfortable in professional settings and call impostor syndrome what it is: limited self-worth caused by unresolved past trauma—whether from childhood, bias and systemic racism, or inherited intergenerational trauma. If we are more transparent about something that at least 70% of us experience, perhaps it could crack open the door to getting more comfortable talking about mental health in the workplace and what is needed to create more psychological safety within our work environments. While the stigma is certainly decreasing, most people are far from being able to share their most human stories and selves with their colleagues and managers.

> Recall the last time you felt like you might be "found out" in a professional context. Describe what that felt like in your body.

## Upper Limiting

If impostor syndrome were a coin, when you flipped it over you'd find *upper limiting*. Upper limiting has been described as a subconscious tolerance cap on how much you will allow yourself to be happy in relationships, physically healthy, wealthy, creative, or successful overall in life.[9] I categorize this as another manifestation of unhealed trauma in adulthood, in the same way I have reframed impostor syndrome.

Upper limiting is another interesting phenomenon because despite the fact that people-pleasers represent at least half of all leaders across industries, how we hold ourselves back is not talked about. If we started to work on the root of our people-pleasing tendencies (trauma), we might begin to set healthier boundaries and care less about approval. Undoubtedly, though, we will encounter upper limiting at some point. It's one thing to be more of our true selves in the world, but it's another thing entirely to break out of our own comfort zones to dream and desire to extents we've never believed were possible for us. For other people, sure. But never for ourselves. It might sound counterintuitive and irrational, but think about it: if we start to edge closer to what we envision for our lives, our safety mechanisms create a hidden barrier to full achievement (uncertainty). If we break the self-imposed cap, we're likely to find it difficult to maintain our reality because our self-limiting beliefs can't tolerate the upleveling.

So long as we avoid doing the work, what we will continue to seek in life is comfort—not growth, fulfillment, and awe. It all comes back to the eternal quest for safety; if we challenge what we believe is possible, the options for how it might play out all seem too risky (failure, humiliation, loss, loneliness). And if we do succeed and are the recipient of newfound abundance, we also fear outshining others (fear of loss of belonging). So the obvious subconscious choice is to keep the ceiling safely in place.

But what if we consciously challenge our self-limitation? What if we commit, as Gay Hendricks puts it, to "thrive uninterrupted?"[10] Though it can be challenging to identify when and why your upper limit problem is online, there are some ways to shine the light on the underlying fears and beliefs about what we are entitled to or capable of achieving. From there, you not only dream bigger, but get more comfortable with receiving.

- **Awareness and recognition:** Notice patterns when you begin to feel uncomfortable, anxious, or fearful when things are going well, and you begin to self-sabotage.
- **Understand your limiting beliefs:** Explore the beliefs that are causing you to consider self-sabotaging thoughts or behaviors. These could be about your worthiness, capability, or what you think is even possible. Visit **MyHealingMenu.com** for modalities that can assist with greater understanding.
- **Reframe your beliefs:** Once you understand your limiting beliefs, work to reframe them into more empowering beliefs. Instead of "I'm not worthy of this success," think, "I am capable and deserving of all the success related to this and beyond."
- **Expand your comfort zone:** Start by setting slightly bigger goals and increasing your capacity to handle incremental increases in success and happiness.

- **Practice mindfulness:** Stay present in the moment, which can help you realize when you're hitting your upper limit and enable you to course-correct before you can even begin to self-sabotage.
- **Prioritize self-care:** Take care of your physical, emotional, and mental health. Self-care is essential in handling the stress and discomfort that can come with pushing past your upper limits.
- **Seek support:** Trust your own intuition, and don't be afraid to seek help. A trauma-informed coach, mentor, therapist, shaman, or other healing practitioner can be invaluable in helping you navigate and overcome your upper limit problem.

This is not an overnight process; it requires patience, perseverance, and kindness toward yourself. All of the so-called failures or times when you've held yourself back from success, growth, and love might finally come into focus. The reasons for your self-sabotage might begin to make sense, leaving you to feel more empowered in the present, more sure about your future, and more excited for what could unfold over the rest of your life.

When have you capped yourself when engaging with financial goals, a dream project, a romantic relationship, or something else?

Why do you think you couldn't allow yourself to experience a greater degree of success?

# 15

## The Value of Nothingness

THE SHAME AND embarrassment I carried for failing the friends and family who invested in the Holistic Option had an upper hand on me. Inside, I was consumed by feelings of worthlessness. The self-importance of my reputation and how others perceived my lack of financial responsibility confirmed that my mother had been right about me all along. It took years for me to purposely delve into the emotions surrounding that experience, to open up to the idea that I was not a failure as a human being, but that the disruptive concept was ill-timed in many ways.

What I had never considered, though, was that by founding a second company just two years after my mother exited my life, and only three years into running my marketing agency, one business was not enough. I had to start a second company to prove my worth—and disprove that my mother's decision to walk away was related to my value as a person. Because that abandonment was simultaneously traumatizing and retraumatizing, it fell right into the framework I talked about in Chapter 1. In my subconscious mind, the way I went about ensuring the safety of my ego was through the lens of the third receptacle: "I have to work harder: *I'll get it perfect next time; maybe then she'll love me.*"

If we dive even deeper, back in 2006 this particular business in the emerging industry of holistic healing and wellness was an external manifestation of the healing I needed. In a conversation with business therapist and mindset coach Nicole Lewis-Keeber, I saw the counter side of that realization: if I was the one creating an entire company based on healing and well-being, then I must be the good one and my mother must be the bad one. That felt like ego protection, too. In her own zone of genius, my colleague built on this: "The idea that other people invested their money in your company signaled to your ego that you must be worth investing in."[1] She continued:

> There are times when we can be compelled to start or use a business to try to disrupt, disprove, rebel against, or confirm what someone has messaged about us in our formative years. As many adults subconsciously rail against the idea that they are not smart enough, valuable enough, or even on the radar of a primary caregiver, just as many re-pattern their trauma—via their leadership position—to confirm what they subconsciously believed to be true all along. Like confirmation bias or self-sabotage, failure becomes more evidence of the false narrative that they are worthless, unintelligent, or destined not to matter. What we desperately want is a new ending, but the challenge is that we bring the same characters to the movie and our negative inner dialogue is still present, challenging and questioning us every step of the way. The inner child in us thinks, "Okay, this time is going to be different." But if we haven't done the healing work to arrive at a meaningful level of understanding about ourselves yet, our trauma patterns will continue to put the same people and scenarios in play every single time.[2]

In addition to this gold, I also took from the conversation that trauma and intuition can live in the same body *and* inside of the same experience. With our intuitive skills, we try to see around corners—and in the realm of business, that is called *disruption*. The most disruptive founders have likely been the most traumatized individuals because they've had to hone their craft of foresight and get ahead of narratives. In a way, it is the crack in the clay vessel that lets the light of consciousness in.

## Posttraumatic Growth Versus Resilience

As we find freedom within ourselves after trauma, some might also call us *resilient*. Instead of the toughness it takes to withstand or bounce back quickly from a challenging experience, *posttraumatic growth* is a horse of a different color. "Posttraumatic growth is a process, and the outcome of this process is positive change in five different domains of life: opportunity, relationships with others, personal strength, greater appreciation of life, and change in belief system of life."[3]

Coined in the 1990s by psychologists Richard Tedeschi and Lawrence Calhoun, posttraumatic growth, or PTG, can be a natural occurrence, or it "can be facilitated in five ways: through education, emotional regulation, disclosure, narrative development, and service."[4] These act as another menu of sorts to better understand how we can embody vulnerability:

- **Education:** Understanding the psychological impacts of trauma can help us anticipate and recognize our own reactions and growth. Books, online resources, or discussions with knowledgeable individuals can all contribute to understanding the psychological impacts of trauma.
- **Emotional regulation:** Developing strategies to effectively manage and express our range of emotions can be achieved through self-taught mindfulness techniques, daily meditation, yoga, or through certain physical activities like jogging or swimming to help release emotion or calm the mind.
- **Disclosure:** Openly communicating about our traumatic experiences with trusted friends, family, or within supportive communities, such as online forums or local support groups, can be beneficial to our growth. It also serves as a way to get more comfortable with vulnerability. Speaking about our trauma can reduce feelings of isolation and can offer new perspectives that aid in the process of integration.
- **Narrative development:** Developing a personal narrative about our traumatic experiences helps to integrate it into our life story. This could be done through journaling, creating art, or even composing music. It allows us to make sense of our experiences

in a way that acknowledges the trauma but also highlights our strength, ingenuity, and inner wisdom.

- **Service:** Participating in service-oriented activities can greatly facilitate PTG. This might include volunteering with a local cause, raising awareness about issues related to our trauma, or providing support for others who've experienced similar events. Service provides a sense of purpose and can transform a negative experience into a catalyst for positive change for others.

As we get comfortable with opening ourselves, we reach new levels of consciousness—where we're able to observe and accept ourselves as we share our interior experiences with those in our lives, and perhaps even more publicly, with the world. There are untold amounts of growth available from the healing process and there are tools that we take with us. When we don't share our experiences, when we don't allow ourselves to embody vulnerability as a newfound default, we lose out on the opportunity to show others what's possible.

Embodying vulnerability offers another benefit in that we start to see how our masked identity no longer serves us. We start to receive that our experiences resonate, more common than we had imagined. Inside of surrender is the realization that we are not alone, nor are we an anomaly. We can then begin to grasp that we are not our thoughts, our behaviors, or the conditioning that informed our persona. We are no longer our identity.

We are perfect as we are, and we are also nothing. The value is in holding these two views as coexistent as we release preprogrammed attachment to the ego. Here, the *value of nothingness* is fascinating for those of us who lead from the fertile soil of trauma integration. From a Buddhist perspective, if we heal a core wound of worthiness, we might discover that we are nothing but pure consciousness. When the body is healing, the mind can be emptied of attachment, and we can finally feel free. This freedom is not a void or lack, but rather an expansive, infinitely potential space. It is a presence full of the unknown, full of possibility and existence beyond our previous understandings. Healing does not discard our past experiences; rather, we integrate them into a deeper, fuller understanding of our place in the universe. We become observers; we can notice our thoughts and emotions, rather than being held captive by them.

This practice of embodied vulnerability and release allows us to tap into the power of presence and authenticity. As we strip away the layers of ego, we connect more deeply with others and with the world around us. We begin to see and appreciate the interconnectedness of all things, and our role in this vast, intricate web of existence. This transformation is our ultimate gift—to ourselves, to others, and to the world. It is in this paradox of nothingness and everything that we find true freedom, inner peace, and purpose.

# 16

---

# The Art of Implementation

THE WAY WE implement vulnerability as leaders requires us to speak up and make changes to the systems that we have either inherited or that we have developed ourselves. That's easier for—and more accessible to—some leaders than others. It would be a disservice if I didn't acknowledge that vulnerability comes at a different cost for those who are white, compared to those who are Black, Brown, and/or Queer.

When it comes to the art of modeling vulnerability as leaders, we first need to fully understand the role that *psychological safety* plays. No one wants to be activated by someone else's share. No one wants to be punished or humiliated for asking questions, raising concerns, sharing ideas, or making mistakes. Yet that is often what happens to people from underestimated communities, regardless of their leadership role or status.

Dr. Carey Yazeed explains, "Before a person of any race can begin to embrace vulnerability and break their silence, two elements are needed: trust and safety. These elements are achieved when belonging, a core human need has been established within the environment. When humans have a sense of trust and safety we feel free to present our authentic selves; opening up and sharing who we truly are with those around us."[1]

The process of creating such an environment takes work, but it is essential for the growth and development of the leaders, the team,

143

and any external resources that might be brought in to work with the people within the organization.

## Valuing Vulnerability on the Stage

Through Consciousness Leaders, the world's most diverse and equitable speakers agency, my team and I represent people of color from across the globe, as well as those in the LGBTQIA+, disabilities, and military veteran communities for paid speaking engagements. I work very closely with those who boldly share their own stories on stage. I see firsthand how some people leaders still request that a speaker or workshop facilitator include a personal anecdote about their lived experience, but want to *pay them in exposure* instead of compensating them appropriately.

When we receive emails from these prospective clients stating that "there is no budget," I immediately hear, "We do not value this person or their lived experience enough to pay them." After the anger recedes, I immediately feel empathy for the people inside of their organization because if leadership is not willing to pay an expert for the value they bring to an event, I can guarantee they are not supporting their employees well. This isn't about one or two organizations within a particular sector either. The reality is that most people in positions of power do not consider or value the experiences of those who don't look like them. The issue is systemic and has been the unchallenged default for far too long.

So let's challenge it. If you do professional speaking of any kind as a leader—and you agree to speak for free—you are not only doing yourself a disservice but you are also inadvertently making it more difficult for other professionals to get paid. Expertise and experience are one thing; the vulnerability and courage it takes to share those publicly is another. Even if the engagement is for a client, puts you in a room full of ideal clients, and you're blatantly told that you'll be shortlisted for a future paid engagement, kindly mention that accepting engagements without pay works directly against equity for all. (Financially, you might be able to speak for free, but that is not the case for most speakers from underestimated communities.) Maybe you'll change some minds, but at least you'll know you did the right thing and the closer we'll get to organizations paying people for their expertise and lived experience.

## Redefining Systemic Vulnerability

By now we know that high-conscious leadership is built on at least two fundamentals: the self-awareness that comes with trauma integration and the embodiment of vulnerability. What we haven't yet talked about is leveling the playing field. Those in power in America (mostly cis/het/white people) are made aware of inequities and afforded the option to rethink the systems that keep us locked into this misaligned and imbalanced paradigm—or not. That requires self-awareness, vulnerability, and courage, but what is the cost of not using one's power to help bring about change?

*Systemic vulnerability* refers to the conditions that threaten the sustainability of a group, organization, institution, or entire ecosystem. However, like most of the counterintuitive concepts of high-conscious leadership, systemic vulnerability is our imperative. Hear me out. When leaders are comfortable being vulnerable—to the point where it influences the culture of their organization—all stakeholders feel safe to ideate and strategize, provide constructive feedback, voice concerns, listen to diverse input, discuss risk factors, and innovate collaboratively on alternative solutions. This includes entire leadership teams, employees, customers, shareholders, and other external stakeholders, such as strategic partners or affiliated parties. In this way, I'm reimagining a different definition, one that serves us in the same way that vulnerability is now regarded as one of the new hallmarks of effective leadership.

To redefine systemic vulnerability in leadership, we would need to transform how we conceive of leadership itself. Beyond a singular focus on the leader, this reimagining views leadership as a collective, participative process. Here, we're pivoting away from the traditional top-down hierarchy and creating a regenerative structure that allows for collaborative problem-solving, prioritizing psychological safety and the freedom of expression.

A culture that welcomes vulnerability is one where leaders allow themselves to be seen in their authenticity and extend the same freedom to their team members. This facilitates conversations that delve deep into problem-solving by allowing room for doubt, uncertainty, and experimentation. Leaders step down from the pedestal of perfection and encourage everyone's contribution to solutions. In these shared spaces, there's mutual respect for diversity, recognizing the importance of myriad perspectives for rich, innovative solutions. Rather than stifling differences, a culture of vulnerability leverages them as a strength, drawing wisdom from individual experience, and weaving it into the broader tapestry of organizational knowledge.

However, creating such a culture extends beyond inviting and respecting diverse points of view. Leaders who truly embrace vulnerability understand that psychological safety is foundational to this process and fosters creativity and innovation as well as deepens interpersonal connections among team members. When we think about the culture we've created within our organization, is there an invitational space for vulnerability?

- As the leader, do we dictate solutions instead of sharing challenges for collaborative input?
- If we do ask for input, do we notice that our team members raise considerations, suggest alternate potential solutions, or remain silent?
- Do we celebrate the value that comes from diverse points of view, or might we not foster psychologically safe group environments where everyone can express themselves freely and respectfully, without judgment or repercussion?
- Do we offer unbound time for thinking and innovation, or do we signal that our priority is on productivity and profitability?
- Do we offer myriad supportive ways for our team members to learn about one another, work with each other, and develop themselves and their skills?
- Do we convene environments that are as much a place of work as they are a space for growth?

This inclusivity also creates an environment where external stakeholders can express themselves openly and honestly. This opens up possibilities for innovative partnerships and alliances.

By shifting toward this future of leadership, organizations not only thrive in terms of productivity and profitability but also nurture a vibrant, inclusive, and innovative culture that is well equipped to navigate the challenges of a rapidly changing business landscape.

## Breaking Down Barriers and Building Equity

As we work toward systemic vulnerability, we must also acknowledge the current imbalance and build structures that promote equity and inclusivity. Particularly for marginalized groups, vulnerability can feel like a risk, rather than a tool for growth. Leaders first need to recognize systemic barriers, then consciously dismantle them, while simultaneously building structures that validate, value, and equitably reward all voices.

Addressing the unequal cost of vulnerability includes creating an atmosphere of psychological safety—and fair compensation for the emotional labor that people from underestimated communities often undertake when sharing their experiences and perspectives. The devaluation of this work further reinforces systemic inequalities. As leaders, we must ensure that everyone is appropriately rewarded for their contributions.

Embracing systemic vulnerability also means reevaluating how we measure success. It cannot only be about productivity and profitability; it must focus on the well-being, engagement, and growth of all of our team members. In practice, this looks like giving and receiving feedback that is direct and actionable, setting clear expectations, sharing difficult information about the organization, and ensuring that these kinds of conversations take place at every level within an organization—not just among the leadership team or between leaders and employees.

As leaders, it is our responsibility to model vulnerability ourselves. This means openly admitting to mistakes, embracing honest interactions, acknowledging when we do not have all the answers,[2] and being willing to reshape organizational power structures.[3] It's not about exposing weakness, but rather about showing humanity. If you still doubt the connection, success, and power of vulnerability, consider the last time you watched your favorite TED Talk, read a vulnerable post on LinkedIn from someone you respect, or heard someone share their personal story on a podcast. Did you see or hear yourself somewhere in their experience? Did you feel more connected to that person? Did you think about reaching out? That's what your employees, colleagues, and others feel when you're open and transparent. The power of vulnerability is untapped; you are the only one who can let your perception and fear keep you from harnessing its power.

What is one systemic change that you need to make as a leader to embody vulnerability?

# PART
# V
## Care in Action

*"When we focus on ourselves, our world contracts as our problems and*
*preoccupations loom large. But when we focus on others, our world expands."*[1]
—*Daniel Goleman*
*PSYCHOLOGIST AND AUTHOR*

WE'VE TALKED ABOUT the first two fundamentals of high-conscious leadership—*Integrating Trauma* and *Embodying Vulnerability*. The third fundamental won't come as a surprise, but I invite you to think differently about *Leading with Compassion*.

Leading effectively means *caring* for your people, their experiences, and the ecosystem within and surrounding your organization—and then taking action to support them in intelligent ways that benefit the whole. Compassion might sound simple enough as a concept, but you'll quickly determine how divergent needs could make us label this particular relationship as "complicated."

In actively healing, more empathy will naturally surface for us as individuals because we're more easily able to access our own emotions. And, of course, if we have unprocessed trauma, it might be more difficult to stand up for what we believe in when it comes time to take action. As we saw with Fundamental #2, there's a lot of risk in standing up for our values—in being that vulnerable to the potential loss of belonging—which is hardest among leadership teams. Yet, just as with any muscle that we want to build, we've got to do the reps.

In Part V, I'll offer some clarity for the intrinsic differences among sympathy, empathy, and compassion so we're in lockstep as we talk about what I call *compassionate intelligence*. This is especially important for people-pleasing leaders who tend to lean into supporting others, sometimes to their own detriment. From there, I'll cover how compassionate leadership influences how organizations respond in four extrinsic key areas: Stakeholder Experience, Competition, Brand Perception, and Reaction to Social Issues. I wrap up with the systemic changes that need to be made as we transform our intention from leading with a productivity mindset to leading with compassion.

# 17

## Fundamental #3:
## Leading with Compassion

BEYOND SIMPLY UNDERSTANDING those under our stewardship and feeling with them, as conscious leaders we are moved to take action to help our people in some meaningful way. Leading with Compassion, the third fundamental of high-conscious leadership, translates into better support for our employees and the planet through a more conscious approach to doing business—whether you run a charity, a corporation, a country, or a corner store.

Let's delineate among three terms that often get used interchangeably but are not synonymous: sympathy, empathy, and compassion.

### Sympathy

The ability to understand someone's emotional experience, or simply that they are having one, is *sympathy*. Too often, this comes across as having pity or feeling sorry for someone who is suffering, and that doesn't help anyone. While it's better to feel *for* a colleague than *sorry for* a colleague, sympathy is antithetical to effective leadership traits.

## Empathy

Empathy goes beyond the understanding of another's experience and is often described as *feeling with* someone who is having an emotional experience. The work of Daniel Goleman and Paul Ekman breaks empathy down further into three distinct subsets: *cognitive, emotional,* and *compassionate.* These lead to more effective communication about challenging experiences, deeper human connection, and more harmonious relationships in work and life.

- **Cognitive empathy:** Understanding how someone might be feeling and what they might be thinking. It's having a good idea of their perspective, mental models, and the language that will resonate most.[1]
- **Emotional empathy:** Feeling with or sharing the feelings of another person, which offers the ability to bond and develop rapport.[2]
- **Compassionate empathy:** Compassionate empathy combines understanding with feeling and inspires us to take action to help someone in distress.[3]

Empathy is obviously necessary for successful outcomes, regardless of the type, size, or sector of our organization. When empathy is a part of the cultural DNA, people feel connected.

*"With empathy, complex problems become more understandable, teams become more effective, and companies become more nimble."*[4]

**—Michael Ventura**
*APPLIED EMPATHY*

However, empathy is not the end of the story for leaders. In fact, if we were to lead with empathy alone, it would be difficult to make decisions through a holistic lens. While empathetic leadership is necessary to connect and engage with our people, there is a gap left between feeling and doing. And *acting from a place of wisdom* is theoretically why we are in positions of leadership, right?

## Compassion

Healing our own trauma helps us remember the more compassionate parts that we've buried over the years—and to see ourselves as part of our collective family. Beyond sympathy and empathy, *compassion* is understanding, feeling, and being willing to help relieve the suffering of another. The action orientation component is what differentiates it from empathy.

# The Art and Science of Effective Leadership

Not that anyone should have to make a case for kindness, but evidence-based research shows how compassion contributes to the bottom line of an organization. Neuroimaging shows that employees' brains respond more positively to leaders who show compassionate empathy.[5] Employees also experience lower rates of burnout and emotional exhaustion inside of cultures led by a compassionate leaders. In these environments, they also physically show up more often.[6] And we know all too well how burnout and absenteeism detract from our quarterly profit margins.

"Numerous studies show that when leaders are primarily focused on the well-being of their employees, this is a strong predictor of employee job satisfaction, perceived organizational support, loyalty and trust in the organization, and retention," as stated in the *Harvard Business Review*. "It also has been linked with improved employee job performance (by boosting employee motivation), and better team performance."[7]

In a study published in the *Journal of Business Ethics* in 2019, researchers set out to determine if compassionate leadership plays a role in creating more compassionate colleagues. Participants worked in the investment banking sector in London, and the study gathered data on emotional response, presence, kindness, and human experience among employee groups that were each paired with a single leader. The researchers discovered a direct correlation between ethical, compassionate group leaders and citizenship demonstrated by peers. They also found that compassion acted as a bond within the work environment when peers recognized each other's emotional responses as part of the larger human experience. Overall, these findings suggest that ethical leaders "more easily move their followers to become sensitized to peers' setbacks and misfortunes and take action . . . to lessen or relieve their suffering."[8]

Safety to express one's self and the care that ensues creates the bedrock needed for the highest levels of creative collaboration, innovative thinking, and productivity. And since employees are ultimately responsible for the quality and speed at which a work product is delivered, increases in both of these elements in any organization translates into higher revenue and a more sustainable model.

A predicted increase in compassion among leaders in corporate, nonprofit, government, higher education, trade associations, and leadership events is one of the many reasons I founded Consciousness Leaders. After the murder of George Floyd, I had a sense that organizational leaders would come to understand—one way or another—the importance of taking action to ensure that their people were well. And some of them really did, but for others it was short-lived and became clear that it was only out of necessity.

It turns out that when we look at the energy and intention behind compassion, one's motivation matters. Research confirms that self-interest is a strategy killer; kindness cannot be used as a leadership strategy, but must always be rooted in altruism.[9] Doing trauma integration work aids in developing a mentality and lifestyle where giving becomes the default—and not with an expectation of getting anything in return. This brings us back to our True Nature.

As compassionate leaders, we have to make difficult decisions when it comes to knowing how best to be kind to our people—counterbalanced with running profitable organizations. Next, we'll explore how to blend compassion with wisdom to make sound business decisions that everyone can feel good about.

Think about a team member who has shared a personal or professional challenge with you. Was your natural response one of sympathy, empathy, compassion, or something else entirely?

# 18

---

# Compassionate Intelligence

To DECIDE WHAT the next right action is to take in any given leadership situation, we can rely on a combination of intuition, compassionate empathy, and business savvy. We must feel it on the inside before we can apply innate wisdom and move toward it externally. Trusting ourselves and our emotions becomes easier once we begin integrating our past, so a mix of instinct and intellect allows us to embody the third fundamental of high-conscious leadership, Leading with Compassion—and it also allows for healthy boundaries that keep our organizations on the path of sustainability.

Thus, what's required is actually a fluid dance that balances both emotional and logical resources. *Compassionate intelligence* is the wisdom to know when, why, and what support someone needs and the responsibility that comes with offering a rational amount.

The action orientation of compassion likely makes it easier for leaders to understand because we're wired toward solution development. Yet that action, in the form of human support, also needs guardrails to keep people-pleasing leaders from over-indexing, to keep people-controlling leaders from developing apathy, and to ensure our organizations are places where healthy boundaries and clear cultural habits are formed.

## The Spectrum Between Martyrdom and Apathy

If this flow and discernment doesn't come naturally, how do you figure out where you currently sit as a leader and what you need to do to shift? Let's go back to fluidity for a moment; if compassionate intelligence were in the middle of a spectrum, perhaps *martyrdom* and *apathy* might exist on either end.

For People Pleasers, empathy comes easily, and compassion is likely our default. Go too far in this direction, though, and you might take action to the detriment of the organization. When we have unprocessed trauma, our compassion for others can cause us to bleed out, metaphorically speaking. This is where we can fall into the trap of martyrdom and overextend ourselves to an irrational degree. That can cause resentment in you, unnecessary anxiety in your people, and a disruption to your bottom line.

For People Controllers, it might be difficult to overcome the impulse to harden around the suffering of others or resent employees who bring personal issues into the workplace. Many of us have had an authoritative leader or two who conveyed their level of compassion as "Life is hard. We don't have time for that. Let's move on. We have work to do." That only alienates people and makes it clear that you don't care about them, which is one of the leading reasons why workers choose to leave their employers. According to the World Economic Forum with research from McKinsey & Company, "uncaring/uninspiring leaders" was cited as why more than one-third of employees leave. Not far behind that were "unsustainable work expectations," "unreliable/unsupportive colleagues," and "lack of support for health/well-being."[1] It all comes down to caring and support, or being seen and valued, and feeling a sense of belonging. Is it any wonder that that is what people want from the leaders and organizations with which they spend the most time—especially when those reflect the same human needs we had when we were younger?

As a leader, I know it can be hard, even impossible, to ensure that every one of your people feels cared for and well-supported. After all, each of them brings *their wounds* into the way they show up at work, so striving for perfection here, too, is a losing proposition. Some of us might oscillate between martyrdom and apathy on any given day, but compassionate intelligence is a practice that can be a win for all. Instead of striving for perfection, what's more helpful is to strive to ensure that people know you care.

> When you've had an employee, teammate, or group member who needed support, where on the spectrum of compassionate intelligence did you show up?

## Can Compassion Really Be Rational?

At the onset of Part V, I invited you to think differently. Compassionate intelligence requires that we listen and we support, yes, but within a framework of healthy boundaries. Professor of psychology and author of *Against Empathy*, Paul Bloom, encapsulates this as "careful reasoning mixed with a more distant compassion."[2]

As an agency leader, I had a few employees over the years who were neurodivergent or a highly sensitive person (HSP). I recall one team member who asked if he could drive home to change his T-shirt because he wasn't able to concentrate due to the way the cotton felt on his skin. He lived about 30 minutes away, so I was looking at over an hour of paid time—not to mention that he was an hour late to work that day. Now, it was clear that he would be too uncomfortable to be productive, so I had to understand what was happening for him and empathize with his distress. Compassionate intelligence kicked in. I agreed to the shirt swap, and we mutually agreed that he would work two hours later that day and lock up when he left the office. As a leader, was that the right decision? All I know is that I cared about his comfort as much as I cared about our client deadlines, and we had an open conversation as a result. When he returned to the office that afternoon, he had an extra T-shirt in hand to store in his desk drawer in case this ever happened again.

What if you're dealing with an employee who is experiencing something that requires more attention and a type of support that you have not encountered before? Let's use drug addiction for an example. Without judgment, we can zoom out to understand that one of our people is struggling in their life and that drugs serve to help them escape that suffering. We might even recall similar situations where we felt as though we were at our lowest and used other forms of addiction to numb or escape, such as alcohol or overwork. Would you rationally support this employee by paying for their in-patient care from your child's college fund? No. But you might find out what services were available through your healthcare provider and work out a way for them to take medical leave, if that's what their doctor or clinician recommended.

The point is we don't have to choose *between* compassion and rationale. We can listen to understand, we can feel, and we can make rational decisions in support of our people and our organization. Everyone can win, as long as no one is expecting perfection.

## What's in Your Toolbox?

It's also important to have a few other practices at the ready. Compassionate leadership, empathetic listening, and trauma-informed training maximize human potential. When people feel safe, valued, and understood, they do their best work. These tools nurture that environment. Instead of offering support in the form of a solution, most people dealing with a challenge really just want to be heard. When you engage empathetic listening in conversations with team members, it might be helpful to ask early on, "Would you like me just to listen, or would you like me to help you solve this?" This way, each of you is set up for success because your mutual desires and expectations have been made clear, you can proceed knowing what roles you can each step fully into, and neither is likely to walk away frustrated.

It is my opinion that the world would be a very different place if trauma-informed training was required for leaders, regardless of organization type or size. Those I work with experience the power of trauma-informed leadership coaching firsthand and can emulate some of our nuanced work together with their employees, but imagine a world in which all leaders understood trauma and practiced compassionate intelligence with their leadership teams. The ripple effect would likely create a sea change within the walls of office buildings and for distributed teams alike.

A portion of trauma-informed coaching includes the ability to maintain presence, to notice subtle shifts in body language or autonomic function while talking with someone, and to engage in Compassionate Inquiry™. Of course, there's a lot more to study regarding what trauma is, what happens within the body's sympathetic nervous system, and how to recognize its behavioral manifestations. Ultimately, though—and we've seen this in the healthcare industry more than any other so far—"trauma-informed leaders cultivate the conditions for posttraumatic growth through their compassionate presence, understanding of trauma responses, and ability to attune to and hold themselves and team members who are experiencing emotional struggles or distress."[3]

All this is to say, if we were able to track others to the extent where we could empower them to identify what was happening inside, offer a safe space to pause and process, and ultimately decide what action they would take next to best support themselves while remaining accountable as an employee, there would be no limit to the level of innovation, collaboration, and impact our organizations could have.

## A Basic Framework for Compassionate Intelligence

When it comes to applying leadership logic to the emotional endeavor of supporting a person under our care who is suffering, three initial questions come into play:

- *What do they need?*
- *What do I need?*
- *What does the business need?*

There's one more question that gets even less attention than these: *What systemic issues or resistance might I run into in offering support?* We will begin to cover some ways in which you can both shift mindset and take action toward systemic change in Chapter 20.

Know that your human resources department (or person) might attempt to thwart your efforts to lean in with more progressive support. Within organizational systems, their role was designed to be an enforcer of policy and a mitigator of liability versus a protector of employee well-being. Think about the function and reality of HR in your organization right now.

Within every industry, some leaders think of humans as beings and others see workers merely as capital or resources. To address this fracture, many larger organizations have started the reinvention of, or delineation from, human resources departments. In 2006, Google was the first company to rename its HR department to People Operations (POPs) "to separate the bureaucratic implications of 'human capital management.'"[4] Several Fortune 50 organizations have adopted similar name changes or delineations, but it's certainly not mainstream (yet). Generally speaking, while HR is focused on compliance and risk management, POPs "bridges the gap between challenges and solutions. It engages the [leadership] team to the present by offering relevant, relatable, and empathetic answers to an employee's concerns."[5]

## Dismantling Oppressive Systems

Let's also talk about how we might support all staff members through a lens that does not center white, cisgender, and heterosexual identity. That singular intersectionality has been the primary, normative influence on all systems that are currently in place in America, the United Kingdom, and most European countries, among others. We can leverage compassionate intelligence to reflect and recognize our own racism, if we are white leaders—and use our power to dismantle the supremacist systems that we uphold in our HR or POPs departments at present. By the way, if you bristle at the notion that white people are inherently racist or unknowingly uphold patriarchal systems—beyond HR and POPs—I want to clarify that while you might interpret these as a personal character attack or flaw, I do not. In fact, if we are able to hold this understanding, more people might be able to engage in dialogue about racism, gun violence, climate change, and other issues that are inextricably connected. I believe that supremacist views have been inescapable if you have grown up white in America; you would not have been able to avoid the privilege afforded to you, nor would you have been able to avoid benefitting from systems that were designed for your success and the oppression of people of color.

Recognizing our own unconscious biases, privilege, and the ways in which we continue to uphold oppressive systems takes continual self-reflection. Being open to feedback from underestimated groups— and seeing things from their perspective—is an important input for developing compassionate intelligence. All of this helps us understand how certain policies favor some groups over others, but this is not about equality; it's about equity. Ensuring that everyone has what they need to thrive will require adjusting policies and practices, and that also means regularly reviewing and revising those through an anti-racist lens.

As leaders, it is also our job to hold all levels of executives and people leaders accountable. When it comes to compassionate intelligence, we need to walk the talk; why and how to do that follows in the next two chapters.

# 19

## How We Respond Matters

IT's NO SURPRISE that organizations led by compassionate leaders thrive in the long term compared to those with low-conscious leaders at the helm. Recall the list of historical and present-day examples in Chapter 7. That is due in part to a shift in employee mindset and consumer behavior when leaders respond to internal or external situations from a place of support—versus indifference or intolerance. This behavioral change, sometimes seen in either unprecedented sales or a boycott, is the extrinsic evidence of the power of compassion—or the lack thereof.

How we respond matters. Compassion matters. We see this in four key areas, although there are certainly many other ways in which the difference is made obvious: Stakeholder Experience, Competition, Brand Perception, and Reaction to Social Issues. The direct experience that our stakeholders have with our organization, as well as how we talk about and respond to our competitors, influences organizational culture and impacts our external brand perception. How we respond matters most when social issues arise, and the last few years have provided more evidence of that than any prior time in history.

Do you recall how organizations responded to the murder of George Floyd and the Black Lives Matter movement? How sharply that changed course in the few years since, especially as DEI programs were defunded at some state universities and government agencies. When funds in places like Florida, North and South Dakota, Tennessee, and Texas were legally no longer allowed to be used for DEI initiatives at state-funded institutions of higher education, the impact was felt far and wide across all sectors—even for those that weren't fiscally affected. Low consciousness has a ripple effect. At Consciousness Leaders, we had several engagements booked with colleges that lost 100% of their DEI funding overnight. Entire diversity offices evaporated and directors were let go in the name of "anti-wokeness."

What about the overturning of *Roe v. Wade*, which decimated safe and legal access to abortion for employees, their partners, and their families across the United States? (First, I specifically do not use the phrase "reproductive health" here because it is inconsiderate of those who have experienced any form of trauma related to reproduction or the patriarchal ideology that the health of those who can reproduce should be viewed solely through the lens of their ability to do so. Second, I do not use the phrase "women's health care" because it excludes nonbinary and transgender people who also have abortions.) On that note, how about the onslaught of gender-affirming care bans that sent individuals and entire families scrambling to relocate their entire lives? When low-conscious decisions are made at levels that impact huge numbers of people, organizational response comes from the top. Those who lead with self-awareness, vulnerability, and compassionate intelligence tend to respond with integrity—doing the kind thing for people and planet, even when it translates into a short-term financial loss or requires a significant change to long-standing systems. I believe that knowing freedom from control and acting accordingly is who we are at a soul level; whether we flow with or go against our higher selves is what differentiates us, particularly when we hold power. Let's look at these four key areas because how we respond can make or break us and our organizations.

## Stakeholder Experience

As high-conscious leaders, when we talk about putting people first, that includes all of our stakeholders—customers, clients, patients, or other patrons of our products or services, employees or colleagues, investors, and all living elements of the natural environment. The experience of, and impact on, the recipients of what we provide in the world matters a great deal to those who lead with compassion.

To know what others are experiencing, we must ask. And how we communicate our questions—so people understand that we care—matters just as much as the data we're trying to glean. All forms of language, engagement, and emotion matter in assessing the experience of our stakeholders. Conscious leadership includes consideration to this extent: thinking ahead, running scenarios, empathizing with the potential experience of, and impact on, each stakeholder type.

If a customer's experience is well considered, they are more likely to remain loyal and even act as ambassadors. When we make mistakes (because we will), the stakeholder experience also includes how we remedy those missteps. If done with a genuine desire to set things right, people will remember and loyalty might increase to even higher levels.

## Competition

Think of the drama that likely ensues when you or your leadership team learns about a new offering or a new approach being taken by a competitor. Now think about how that slightly frenzied energy trickles down to the rest of your organization. What if you opted not to do that and opened to a new way of being in your industry?

High-conscious leaders do not see competition; they view others within and outside their own industry as potential collaborators. Imagine how much further we could get if we were less concerned about hoarding information and putting others out of business. That win-lose thinking is a waste of precious energy, and it doesn't leave anyone feeling good at the deepest level. A related issue is what happens psychologically within some of our employees. We can limit their creativity and ingenuity instead of working together to solve issues that could positively impact a greater audience. Think of this negative impact as *creative contraction* instead of *imaginative expansion*.

## Brand Perception

You know the adage—a brand is not what you say about it, but what everyone else perceives it is. Consider a brand like X (formerly known as Twitter), and how it has dwindled under the low-conscious leadership of Elon Musk. The day he made his offer to buy Twitter, Musk said,

"This is just my strong, intuitive sense that having a public platform that is maximally trusted and broadly inclusive is extremely important to the future of civilization." He even talked about his vision for it being the expansion of "the scope and scale of consciousness."[1] Ever since then he has proceeded to ensure the exact opposite—best encapsulated by his post on X from December 15, 2023: "DEI must DIE."[2]

The Spanish fast-fashion brand Zara triggered a boycott and protests outside of its retail stores just before the end of 2023 for a campaign that many people felt was insensitive. Instead of the intended depiction of a messy sculptor's studio with busts, the images felt far too close to what we were seeing every day from the media in Palestine—corpses wrapped in white plastic amidst rubble. Even though the brand justified the campaign as being photographed before the conflict erupted, Hamas's attack on Israel occurred exactly 60 days prior to the launch of the ads. There was plenty of time to change course, but a defensive and deflated apology almost seemed to make matters worse for brand.

In stark contrast, take the brand perception of Patagonia since its CEO, Yvon Chouinard, announced that the profits from the business would be transferred to a charitable trust in which Earth is legally the sole shareholder and beneficiary. It's an admirable move, and he joins the CEO of Ecosia, who did the same thing back in 2018. Kristine McDivitt Tompkins, former CEO of Patagonia for 20 years, said, "I believe this plan that [Chouinard] and his family helped create is tectonic. It will make the company more competitive and its employees around the world will forever be empowered by purpose."[3]

I like the idea of considering the boldest moves first and working from there. Brand perception is based solely on actions—and the feelings, emotions, and/or alignment with those actions. It's a lot easier for us as leaders to do right by all of our stakeholders, especially in moments when that seems the hardest.

## Reaction to Social Issues

Things quickly get complicated in the land of low-conscious leadership. Brand perception and reaction to social issues have a clear crossover—whether the subject is climate change, systemic racial injustice, wage inequality, the mental health epidemic, revocation of abortion, dissolution of rights for LGBTQIA+ people, gun violence, or genocide, to name a few. We know these challenges are intertwined with related societal issues, many of which are rooted in a supremacist mindset. How leaders and organizations respond matters. The precedent has been set that as part of a brand's purpose, it should take a stance on relevant social issues—particularly if the issue aligns strongly with its core values, as well as what its clients or customers care deeply about. The pressure to take a stand on hot-button social, political, moral, and cultural issues comes from consumers, employees, and investors alike. Saying nothing is no longer an option.

In the era of the conscious consumer, those who purchase the very products and services we sell consider the environmental and social components of our brands—and the individual stance we take as chief executives. And the results are in. When low-conscious leaders, such as the CEO of Goya, the owner of Chik-fil-A, and the CEO of MyPillow, prove they are on the wrong side of history, their companies eventually fall under attack from all sides and might ultimately fail in the long term. Research says that about two-thirds of consumers worldwide will choose to buy or boycott a product or entire organization because of its stance on environmental, social, or political issues. The president and CEO of global communications firm Edelman, Richard Edelman, explains, "Brands are now being pushed to go beyond their classic business interests to become advocates. It is a new relationship between company and consumer, where purchase is premised on the brand's willingness to live its values, act with purpose, and if necessary, make the leap into activism."[4]

Have you personally responded or remained silent on social issues? How has your organization responded, or not? And do you know how that action or inaction has been perceived by your stakeholders?

# 20

---

# A Shift in Intention

SINCE THE INDUSTRIAL Age, the focus of organizational culture has been on productivity and profitability. This has historically been to the detriment of the human beings inside those organizations. Leaders who attempt to grow their revenue by eschewing the pick-two rule of the Golden Triangle—better, faster, or cheaper—sacrifice the well-being of their people in the name of their own ego and shareholder profits. Eventually, the whole system becomes unsustainable because the remaining stakeholders experience a lack of consciousness and integrity in the intent behind the product or service. That leads to employee turnover, negative reviews from customers, and declining revenue or share prices for owners and investors in the long term.

The evolution from productivity as our primary intention to employee well-being is at the heart of high-conscious leadership. This shift ensures that our people are well supported, which positively impacts all aspects of workplaces, from internal culture and competitive advantage to market share and the bottom line.

This transformation of intention also means that the holistic systems we have created must be adapted to consider the physical, mental, emotional, and spiritual aspects of all peoples. If we don't change the systems in which we operate, we cannot deem it consciousness. Liberating people to create on their own terms allows for greater innovation. Some examples include centering remote or hybrid work options, reducing the number of days in the workweek, and providing access to more holistic, innovative, and progressive wellness programs and resources—including access to abortion and gender-affirming care if it has been revoked in the state in which you operate. These require systemic modifications and, at times, an outright overhaul and redesign of existing systems. Naturally, questions arise:

1. How do leaders make this shift in mindset first?

2. Where do we begin to influence the systemic changes that must be made to best support our people?

To set the context for how I propose these questions be answered, let's start with the foundational beliefs I hold.

First, organizations are run by people; they do not operate or function independently. They are not entities that can think for themselves, nor do they possess rationale or have emotions. Therefore, hiding behind what we have normalized as *business logic*, in any sector, is simply a way for most leaders to dodge the responsibility with which they were entrusted.

Second, valuing one's self and trusting one's intuition are imperative to having the courage it takes to lead from a place of integrity. Therefore, mindset shifts require inner healing work to rewrite the *not enough* stories that we inherited from our upbringing.

If we can agree on those, then we might be able to agree on a few more things, too. There are a lot of highly intelligent and deeply caring human beings who live on this planet. Some of them find themselves in positions where they have the potential to make a sweeping impact, but for a multitude of reasons they feel paralyzed. There must be another option than this: in every organization, the majority suffer to survive while the few writhe in riches and justify their action (or inaction) with the weight of responsibility they carry.

We need a seismic shift in intention. It starts with every single leader who knows, in their body, that this is not the future of work. The most successful among us don't believe that we are enough or will ever have enough. That is unintegrated trauma talking, and that has kept us frozen inside of systems that we know are wrong—ripe with inequity and reducing our earthly kin to ruin in every corner of the globe. What we need is a new systems approach that is rooted in *being and doing energy*. In simple terms, I see *being* as mindset (a shift in how we think and what we believe about our contributory role in the world) and *doing* as action (a shift in our willingness to initiate and drive change).

## 14 Tenets of Eco-Leadership

To shift mindset, leaders must first assess the reality of the status quo—who benefits and who suffers. We cannot look away from what we will see. When we use or accept adages like "It's just business" or "This is just the way things have always been," we perpetuate the suffering that is caused inside of systems. Our systems. The goal is to move from an ego-centric to an *eco-leadership mindset*, that is, one that favors *the relational ecosystem*—by decolonizing the mind and replacing the inflexible status quo with systems rooted in an ethical approach toward human-powered organizations.[1] This lays the foundation for conscious decisions that consider the well-being of all people, the organization, and the planet. It's a continuous process of self-work and unlearning old paradigms. Here are the seven tenets of *developing an eco-leadership mindset*:

1. **Self-Reflect.** Identify limiting beliefs about productivity, profits, business priorities, and so on. Take time for introspection to understand your own biases, blind spots, and limitations. Be willing to acknowledge your mistakes and areas for growth.

2. **Gain Perspective.** Immerse yourself in books, podcasts, courses, and the like on conscious leadership principles, personal development, and people from other cultures and life experiences to augment empathy and compassion.

3. **Get Vulnerable.** Expressing humanity with employees and stakeholders allows us to relate to people first as humans. Create an open culture where people feel safe to challenge your ideas and give input. Listen without ego to critiques and different viewpoints.

4. **Speak Up.** Those who are against equity in any form are the loudest of the low-conscious leaders. The people who are

for it are afraid to speak up; however, theirs are the voices we need to hear. The choice point is the mindset from "I'm afraid of what might happen or what others might think if I advocate for what I believe in" to "What is the impact of my silence on people and more-than-human kin?"

5. **Develop Systems Thinking.** Look at the interconnections between things rather than linear cause-and-effect. Think about how you are part of larger systems and how each of your actions has a ripple effect.

6. **Let Go.** Redirect yourself away from ego-driven goals, self-aggrandizement, and status. Align goals on purpose and contribution rather than personal gain.

7. **Focus on the Greater Good.** When making decisions, consider how your actions will impact others. Beyond yourself and even your organization, make choices that benefit the larger community and inspirited world.

Once you're in the frame of mind to shift intention, the next step is to create the necessary changes within the systems that are not serving the organization's greater purpose. Building upon the previous list, here are the seven tenets of *taking eco-leadership action*:

8. **Educate All Leaders.** C-Suite leadership teams, directors, and managers should be trained on conscious leadership principles and benefits. If we want employees to experience consistency and follow-through, everyone must receive the same information, participate in experiential learning, and dialogue about their discoveries, challenges, and celebratory wins.

9. **Communicate Consciously.** Openly explain the "why" behind all changes to gain buy-in and adoption will be fairly seamless. Provide space for all questions, concerns, feedback, and takeaways.

10. **Enlist Support.** Partner with conscious leadership coaches and consultants to help leaders and entire workforces transform workplace culture together.

11. **Engage All Stakeholders.** As disability rights activists have reminded us since the 1990s, "nothing about us without us." With each stakeholder at the table, new policies can be decided collaboratively by those who will be affected by that policy. Depending on the organization size and sector, that might also mean investors, consumers, Indigenous elders, and climate science representatives as well.

12. **Redefine Success.** Measure impact on employee well-being as the priority above traditional organizational metrics. If your people feel healthy, safe, and fulfilled, productivity, quality, revenue, and profit margin goals will be realized.

13. **Test and Iterate.** Pilot new policies and gather feedback from employees; create an environment of understanding, flexibility, and iteration as you go.

14. **Collaborate.** Share your findings, challenges, wins, and overall experiences with other conscious organizations both within your industry as well as outside of it. Together, you can determine best practices for systemic change to share with organizations that are slower to adopt this new way of being.

The key is maintaining compassion, courage, and patience throughout the process. It's an evolutionary journey that requires ongoing learning and adaptation. The plethora of rewards—on the individual, organizational/cultural, environmental, and societal levels—make it well worth the effort.

Now that you've gained insight into what's required to lead with compassion, what commitments will you make to yourself going forward? To your people?

# PART

# VI

# The Great Remembering

*"The purpose of life is to discover your gift. The work of life is to develop it. The meaning of life is to give your gift away."*[1]

—*David Viscott*
*PSYCHIATRIST AND AUTHOR*

THIS LAST PART moves us toward discomfort to revolutionize healing for ourselves, others, and the systems in which we operate. If we want to feel fulfilled, a deeper sense of connection, and success on a soul level, we must reclaim our relationships and rebuild broken institutions.

Wherever we are in our leadership journey, we constantly choose what type of direct and indirect impact we will have. When we choose revolution, a whole new way of being becomes available to us. As we engage with the final of the four fundamentals, I invite you to think about yourself, your family, and your communal purpose in a new light. You have the ability and capacity to redirect your own life, to leverage your power on behalf of those who cannot speak for themselves, and to blow the doors off systems that never served us all.

The thing is, you already know how to do this. Contrary to what so many people want you to believe, innate leadership is not a skill to be learned or a framework to be followed; it's a way of being that is encoded in our composition. There is no manual. There is only a deep knowing.

But trauma makes us second-guess even efforts based on altruism. So many of us stop ourselves from answering difficult questions or taking courageous action because we're solely focused on what we might find out, all the reasons why we might fail, or the potential discomfort we might feel if we succeed.

When we, as high-conscious leaders, focus on the difference we can make in other people's lives, we are more likely to go out of our way to help. In fact, our innate desire to support others is so strong that if we were to measure the power of altruistic motivation, we are 120% more likely to take action if we know it will make someone else in our life happy.[2] We have long known that benefiting others plays a vital role in both individual and societal well-being, but scientists have recently made a fascinating discovery. A part of the brain—the anterior cingulate cortex gyrus, or ACCg—lights up when most of us empathize, choose to help others, and exert force to benefit them. Interestingly, those same neural mechanisms do not activate at all when we are the beneficiary of the same effort.[3] As we have been pulled further away from our original, kindhearted nature by individual and collective trauma, caring for other lives or considering the environment has devolved from an absolute honor to something that requires thought as to whether it's worth the effort.

As we continue down the path of self-inquiry, observing ourselves as leaders who embody vulnerability and act with compassion, our natural inclination will be to create more positive impact in every corner of life. To help the people under our leadership and those who are important to them. To ensure that our decisions are environmentally reparative and regenerative. To equally distribute the power we wield.

A flock of geese flies overhead. Close your eyes to listen. Open them, and remember.

# 21

---

# Fundamental #4:
# Lighting the Way

By this point, I think we can all agree that trauma integration is our leadership responsibility. It is the thing we own as individuals for the greater benefit of ourselves, and for everyone and everything outside of us. Lighting the way starts with the self—leaning into the uncomfortable questions we have avoided for a lifetime. We might not want to *go there*, but moving through our trauma is the only way forward; that's the *revolt* in this leadership revolution.

Most of us define success by our own achievements, how well we provide for our families, and perhaps the achievements of our immediate family members. But most of these metrics are rooted in societal comparison, and it's been said that *comparison is the thief of joy*. Leaning into the discomfort means putting all of that aside and asking yourself questions like these:

- Did you pursue the things you've achieved because they felt like an inner calling, because of external expectation, or because of a subconscious understanding that you would gain a sense of belonging if you followed a particular life path?
- If you suffer from depression, what might you be pushing down emotionally? If you have anxiety, what stories are you making up? What fears are you fueling? If these symptoms ever lead you to

feel like you're not enough or that you're too much, do you want to feel differently?

- If you tend to numb yourself with (even occasional) forms of addictive behavior, do you want to be liberated from feeling like you constantly need to fill a void?
- Are you aware of the trauma you're passing on to your children, employees, or others in your life? If this is new information, do you feel compelled to cease doing more harm to the people you care about?
- Do you continue to blame someone or something for your misfortune, mental state, or life's trajectory? Do you ever feel like you're just surviving? If so, are you ready to take real ownership of your past, present, and future?

Every one of us wants to feel like we matter, that we are loved, and/or that we belong. I promise you that the discomfort in these questions is temporary, as healing allows you to see yourself from outside of your *lens of victimization*. While that might be hard to read for some, that lens is the very thing keeping you stuck, smaller than you were destined to be, and focused on self-satiation—to the detriment of those who could benefit from your gifts. To put it plainly, the more you help others, the better you feel.

## The Epidemic of Not-Enoughness

The intention is not to eliminate the ego but to assign its proper role and to make clear its responsibilities—strategy, logistics, and problem-solving—in the name of unearthing our own gifts so that we can be generous with them. Internally, once we are no longer driven by the ego, we arrive at a place where we find joy and are driven by the reward of helping others; it's no longer about the legacy we might leave. We become less obsessed with making millions, the power that comes with social status, and what all of that says about our human worthiness.

We've talked a lot about wounded leaders, and I want to offer an ever more holistic view of the extractive qualities of People Controllers (and unconscious consumers, for that matter) because I think it's important to underscore the place from where they are operating—and how we might be able to help each other heal.

As we know, the ones among us who take more than they need or give—they lie, make decisions that oppress others, and act against the consensus—are simply wounded children in adult clothing. We see this illustrated within family dynamics, in major corporations, and on today's political stages—and it's all in the name of filling the void of *not being enough* or *never having enough*.

Each time we unconsciously make choices that harm other beings, leave a larger carbon footprint, or ensure that we get more so others get less, our wounds are at play. That scarcity mindset comes back online. But taking only what we need is an act of resistance. If we stop and pause to make more emboldened choices out of integrity and love, we can shift the narrative away from individualism toward communal healing. We can put an end to the epidemic of not-enoughness.

Since healing and the integration of trauma is lifelong work, we never arrive at a destination. Instead, our mindset, feelings, and behaviors constantly shift and move ever closer toward integrity—for ourselves, for the well-being of others, for the sustainability of our organizations, to be in right relationship with the land, and for our impact on future generations of all beings. The entrepreneurial spirit will always thrive in generative environments, so when we integrate our emotional history, become comfortable with vulnerability, and lead with compassion, our natural next step will be to participate in the *alchemy* of relationship. We shift internally from the desire for power to the embodiment of love. Similar to the change in intention I talked about in Chapter 19, moving from power to love is a shift in motivation from "me" to a much bigger "we." In other words, by giving yourself the energy and love that you deserve, you generate energy and love for the community—as close or far-reaching as you define it.

Where might there be an opportunity for you to shift from the desire for power to the embodiment of love in your leadership role?

Name five ways you can you participate in the alchemy of relationship in your life, work, volunteerism, and play.

## Disrupting Leadership Norms

For me, community is the felt sense of fellowship when we share core values, goals, or interests with others. So what do we need to keep in mind when lighting the way? In holding space for others—regardless of whether they are just like us or entirely different from us—return on investment (ROI) cannot be a motivating factor. We must be confident and have faith that this approach to organizational leadership will pay long-term dividends in many ways that cannot be measured. Nor do they need to be. We need to let go of antiquated methods of success measurement. This is part of a larger, disruptive ideology that I'll talk about in Chapter 22. Essentially, we move away from a production-performance approach and toward conscious, anecdotal, and relational feedback. If we need numbers for shareholders to chew on, year-over-year revenue and profitability are great indicators of an organization's psychological safety and overall culture. If we want to change the world, we need to model healing and re-membering. This requires a far more relational approach to how we "do business"—no matter the type of workplace.

## Seeing the Whole Human

First, leaders who are doing trauma integration work create the opportunity for more healing in that they begin to pivot to *leading the whole person*. Part of returning to our natural state of consciousness is wanting others to see themselves as whole, too.

In most workplaces, we've relegated our people to one-dimensional definitions of themselves. We need to see the heart before the hard skills, not the other way around. Our bias has been to view employees as fit for a particular position. If not, we enter them into a period of performance review, the make-or-break timeline where they must prove themselves capable of doing a job. What if we took the time to understand how the output might be made more easeful? What if we had a better understanding of how they worked best, what support would facilitate their success, what past or present personal challenges they might be dealing with, and what other intersectional aspects of their being might be engaged in the work?

## Partaking in Sacred Relationship

Secondly, we cannot talk about lighting the way without referring to the depth and quality of relationships that develop when we do. We often leave spirituality out of conversations, but when we hold space for the healing, we create meaningful and honorable partnerships. These relationships are sacred, something that the Indigenous view holds so dearly. When we make the conscious choice to engage in *relationship as a sacred path*, we decide the intention by which we are guided. In practice, this could include beginning in-person or remote meetings with an honest check-in about how each person is arriving to the space, as opposed to jumping right to what needs to be done—*more being, less doing*. It might mean starting conversations with a short, guided meditation to ground and ensure that each person's nervous system is calm and operational. It could also mean creating a shared agreement at the onset that all participants will be fully present and engage in active listening.

## Being Self-Affirming

It might seem counterintuitive, but I'd underscore how we've found ourselves here in the first place. Childhood trauma destroys our trust in the relationship to our self, to other humans, and to our sense of place in the world; it is in this destruction of trust where our disconnection to being and beings begins. To light the way for others, we must cultivate an abiding trust with our primary partner—our self. After all, how can others trust us if we cannot trust ourselves?

In practice, this could mean making continuous promises to yourself and then keeping them, and affirming your own worthiness and value through self-talk that is encouraging rather than negative. Once you become self-resourced, seeking approval in workplace environments no longer gets in the way of your leadership. That translates into a desire to raise up others because your own needs are being met (by you).

## Elevating and Empowering Others

While I've just offered a few examples, what else might constitute lighting the way for others within a trauma-informed workplace environment?

- **Empathize and act with compassion.** Seek to understand others' experiences and create a psychologically safe environment where people feel comfortable sharing and being vulnerable. Ask questions rather than assume. Don't judge or dismiss trauma, or its impacts.
- **Provide opportunities for voices to be heard.** This could include town halls, focus groups, anonymous surveys to surface issues, and an open-door policy to talk. Actively listen without defensiveness or the need to solve, fix, or even reply right away.
- **Offer mentoring and coaching to nurture emerging leaders.** Recognize the potential in your people. Give them stretch assignments, training, and offer your time to develop their capabilities or hire a coach.
- **Advocate for equity and inclusion.** Make sure people from all backgrounds have seats at the table. Call out biases the moment you see them. Champion initiatives that foster belonging.
- **Role model healthy communication and conflict resolution.** Pause before reacting to regulate before responding. Admit when you're wrong, apologize, and commit to do better. Seek win-win-win solutions. Don't avoid hard conversations. Create a harm repair plan.
- **Promote wellness resources like counseling, coaching, and support groups.** Allow time off as needed, specifically for healing. Be transparent about using these yourself.
- **Celebrate posttraumatic growth and victories.** Praise effort, progress, and adherence to shared agreements. Share credit for successes. Uplift those who find their voice and step into leadership roles as they integrate their own trauma.

The path forward starts with awareness, courage, and compassion from those in charge. By creating a nurturing environment, leaders empower those they lead to gain strength, share their gifts, and play a greater role in creating a better future for the organization and far beyond it. The ripple effect that our own healing creates within healthy workplace environments, employees' families, local communities, regional lands, and for all life on this planet is both moving and immeasurable.

We live feeling more fulfilled by the impact that others are making at micro and macro levels alike.

Early mentorship of emerging leaders is critical. High-conscious leaders inspire others to emulate the ways in which they live and lead; perhaps more important, though, is being open to learning from those who arrive awakened. What younger generations might lack in experience, they bring tenfold in intuition, conviction, and initiative. Communicating with these employees about business goals, organizational vision, and their contributory roles is vital because they are making higher-stakes decisions more autonomously than ever before. For us as leaders, our roles begin to pivot toward a future without us. By elevating others, we light the way for collective success, beginning with those we elevate. The win-win-win is that others are supported in the opportunity to lead, which allows us to distribute the pressure we feel, and the organizational ecosystem becomes stronger and regenerative.

So how does a leader know when it's time to rotate to the back, where resistance is lightest? With geese, it seems that the awareness of the weight of their wings—after expending so much energy—is key to this knowing. Beyond that self-awareness, when those we lead honk louder from behind, we must heed what they are communicating. We must listen when people tell us what they need. We must listen when the earth asks us to be in right relationship.

How will you find the courage to create a new level of leadership that inspires healing in others and generates impact in the world?

# 22

# Essential Work

INHERENTLY, WE KNOW how to heal ourselves. When we are ill or injured, our bodies remedy without thought. We are living proof that when we are unwell, balance must be restored, and so it is. No matter the size of our "T," everyone is capable of restoration to wellness. We have simply forgotten how essential it is to heal as leaders, so we stay in our pain, rely on survival mechanisms, and make sure we get our share of what's on offer before someone else gets theirs (or gets us). This is the pain tolerance we have subscribed to because somehow it has become easier to live in a state of threat perception than to lean into the discomfort of uncertainty and effort it takes to integrate our emotional and psychological wounds. But leaning in is our responsibility, and you know that now.

Healing will always be about *progress, not perfection.* You need not feel like you must achieve some enlightened state of being, or have reached some destination where all or most of your trauma has been integrated before you can light the way for others. That day might always feel like it's just around the corner, and in waiting for it you'll miss out on opportunities to change other people's lives. We are all actively healing, all the time.

In the movie *Honey, I Shrunk the Kids,* there's a scene where all four children have already been downsized, and they are lost in the lawn of their backyard. The neighborhood lawn mower walks through the gate, starts up the machine, and proceeds to cut the grass. Unbeknownst to him, the shrunken kids are trying to escape the mower's blades and the funnel of air suction caused by their high-speed spinning. Because the characters are so small, the individual blades of grass are enormous and tower over the kids like thick green skyscrapers, blocking out the sun.

I hadn't recalled that particular scene until about a month before I completed the manuscript for this book. It was the first of August, and the tomato plants in my vegetable garden had grown to seven feet tall. Seriously. The beautiful, broad leaves of the delicata squash were taking over the raised beds, and the sugar snap peas were racing up the trellis to beat the giant sunflowers before they bloomed. That night, I was submerged from the neck down in my portable spa tub, which sits in the center of my garden. (My partner is full of genius ideas like this one!) As I soaked, I laughed out loud at the realization: looking at the thick greenery hovering over me I suddenly understood. I was no longer small; I was big. Everything surrounding me was just *bigger*, *more supportive*, and *actively growing*. The reframe of this core memory, the night of my dad's departure, was a joyfully healing moment. Sitting in the womb-like water, I just smiled and thanked each of the plant teachers around me. I channeled a new mantra: "I am the rightful creator of this dream. I am the rightful author of my next chapter. I am, and everything surrounding me is abundant and expansive."

## The Light of Trauma

On the other hand, our planet's capacity for humankind is finite, somewhere between 9 and 10 billion. By 2050, there will be an estimated 9.7 billion people on earth,[1] and before my 70th birthday we will have hit our max. Even young children already sense the imperative that an increased population has on the climate. Much of what holds us back from tending to the earth is that we see the crisis as an insurmountable cause, so who are we to think we can do anything about it? With that self-limiting belief, is it any wonder why we find ourselves on the edge of this cliff?

My intention here is not to overwhelm you, but to evoke a ground rising. As more of us inhabit this beautiful blue marble, we need to commune in ways that have yet to be imagined. In the radical act of healing the past, we will likely see everything through a new lens, our voices might become louder, and our conviction to live and lead with integrity will grow stronger. Once we can identify one thing that inspires movement in our soul—rooted in engaging in healthy relationship for the benefit of others—we will become a part of the solution. In fact, we already are; it just might feel a little ambiguous as to how we turn our pain into gold. When we take personal responsibility for our own healing, we want to restore our world.

Would it make sense if I told you about an urban farmer who grew up with food insecurity as a child, only to find his passion for growing fresh food for his community and running educational programs for kids? In his case, purpose was born from the trauma of not having enough to eat, and his gift is in mitigating that experience for children who are growing up in similar situations. He is driven by the conviction that no child in his community has to go hungry if their families are able to grow some of their food or come to the farm to get items they need. This farmer is unknowingly raising a whole generation to understand how their food is grown and gain a deeper respect for the environment.

What about the educational administrators who were interviewed by Dr. Mills (discussed in Chapter 3)? Each survived sexual abuse during childhood and needed to stay hidden as a means of survival. In their current leadership roles, they go out of their way to ensure that the underestimated employees in their districts are elevated and made more visible. The leaders cannot bear the thought of others feeling unseen—the way they did when they were younger.

It's also why some people are drawn to certain fields. Psychologists typically want to learn everything they can about human development and behavior, especially when dysfunction was so present in many of their own upbringings. Helping others who have experienced trauma offers a way to give others the support they wish they had in youth. Many of those in emergency health services are magnetized to crisis situations and leverage their lived experience to support others on potentially the worst day of their lives. Some public relations professionals, especially those who specialize in crisis management, are naturally gifted at getting ahead of a narrative and tend to have a high tolerance for instability. So the skills they developed due to childhood trauma end up translating well in the communications business. Often, an attraction to a high-stress, dangerous, or PTSD-prone career is unconscious; we don't realize that we are attempting to play out unmet needs from childhood.

And there's my own path, coaching others to heal and therefore lead more effectively. Having been on the receiving end of a lot of physical and emotional abuse, I feel a sense of purpose in empowering leaders to see themselves as whole. That's why I combine leadership coaching with somatic emotional release, Reiki, and my innate gifts of intuition, connection, and love. The energy I put into the world is the same as what I didn't receive when I was younger. I want leaders to know they matter because I didn't feel that way for much of my life.

In these examples, all involved are actively healing from trauma and lighting the way for others because of it. When you take a step back, the design of our lives becomes clear: for those of us who have faced adversity during our youngest years, our responsibility is our own healing, but our contributions in the world are the reward for our brave work.

Looking back at your upbringing, how might you have turned your pain into prowess?

List all the beings who benefit from the work you've done thus far to heal (or will benefit once you begin).

# 23

---

# What We Receive When We Give

MANY TIMES WE don't realize the influence we have on those constellating in and around our lives and organizations. We rarely if ever think about the impact that our leadership style has on our employees' family units, communities, and future generations. Yet many of the relationships I cultivated with my agency employees remained intact long after the acquisition. I've celebrated their engagements and weddings, home ownership, and the births of their children. In March 2022, I was invited to the wedding of a former team member, Gaby, and her fiancé, Nick, who had also done some video production work for our agency. It was a beautiful wedding, relatively small, and I felt honored to be invited.

Gaby's father saw me standing at a high-top table. He asked if I was his daughter's former boss, and I smiled, "You must be Dad. I've heard a lot about you." He hugged me on the spot and proceeded to tell me how grateful he was that, as his daughter's very first employer, I saw the same potential in Gaby that he did. What meant even more to him was how I've continued to support her career over the years. I was always thrilled to do anything I could for her, both personally and professionally. He described the impact that Gaby's success has had on his immediate family and on the extended family of nieces and nephews, who saw her go to college and see her flourishing as she levels up in her career with each courageous step. I had no idea that any of this was happening, so naturally I was moved to tears by his words and profound gratitude.

The experience gave way to my curiosity about how family members of employees might be positively impacted on an epigenetic level when leaders lean in. In Chapter 5, we talked about the negatives of firsthand inheritance of traumatic experiences. Since behavior and environment can change how the body *reads* a DNA sequence, mindset and subconscious inputs make an impact on the molecular level as well. Therefore, positive emotions, mind-body therapies,[1] and witnessing a new level of potential for your own life can alter how your genetic inheritance is expressed just as much as negative inputs can. If we knew that we wielded this wisdom, think about how we could aid in the healing of our own families, inspire healing in the families of those we lead, and actively rebuild the systems that have benefitted us to the exclusion of others. Think about the disservice to the whole when we do nothing.

We want to do the next right thing. Using compassionate intelligence, we think about how we *could* help someone else. Yet most of us suffer from a fear of being seen for our divine gifts, so we end up talking ourselves out of leaning in. Our hearts are in the right place, but the trauma that resides in our bodies often holds us back from lighting the way for others. This is why somatic emotional release is so important; it activates our parasympathetic nervous system, which allows us to return to a homeostatic environment within ourselves.

As I said in Chapter 8: *What if we do it all for the purpose of healing*—ourselves, each other, and the earth? The significant impact we can make as leaders bears repeating, especially when we decide to do the work, get vulnerable, lead with compassion, and light the way. We can raise each other up, higher and higher.

## Native Actualization

Abraham Maslow argued that for adult humans to reach their potential, a linear hierarchy of needs must be satisfied, beginning with basic physiological requirements and safety, love, belonging, esteem, self-actualization, and, finally, transcendence.[2] While I attributed one sentence in Chapter 12 to his motivational theory, I have purposefully chosen not to pay homage to the popular psychologist. Why? Most of what was represented as "a doctrine of discovery and a hierarchical system" was formulated from the teachings of elders from the Siksika (Blackfoot) Nation in Alberta, Canada. Maslow was an industrial and organizational psychologist; as such, he reinterpreted the Blackfeet teachings to better align with an individualistic and capitalistic society.[3] In short, it is the opposite of the wisdom he was generously given. More specifically, the primary difference between the Indigenous perspective and Maslow's hierarchy was that *self-actualization* (the fulfillment of one's potential)[4] was the foundation of being in community for Native American peoples, while his model placed it at the top of a pyramid, just below *transcendence* (the highest level of human consciousness).[5] According to Blackfoot wisdom, *community actualization* and *cultural perpetuity* (also called *the breath of life*) transcend the self.[6] In other words, to be part of the continuity of all life on earth is the highest form that a person can attain.

This major difference provided further misdirection of our human species away from one another at a precise time in history when war gave way to the baby boom and consumerism. In an interview on the subject, Dr. Sidney Stone Brown said, "I hope that . . . everyone will look at Maslow's hierarchy as something that supported capitalist thinking and belief systems, allowing only 5% of the population to be actualized, when in reality, in Native populations, Indigenous worlds, everyone has a purpose. Everyone is brought here for a reason. We are all to make a contribution, and, based on altruistic values give back to the world."[7]

Maslow is not to blame for hyper-consumerism or climate change. Nor is he the only psychologist who learned from Native peoples without giving credit where it was due, or honoring their depth of wisdom enough to keep it intact. Erik Erikson received the basis for his theory of child development by studying the Oglala Lakota people,[8] and Carl Jung was directly trained by Hopi elders.[9] In fact, after Jung's first encounter with an elder known as Mountain Lake, he wrote about white people, "Knowledge does not enrich us; it removes us more and more from the mythic world in which we were once at home by right of birth."[10] As he learned more about the harmony that appeared throughout many cultures, the primary focus of his work was a spiritual urge toward unity.

Particularly in America, our default has perpetuated divide through othering—a far distance from cultural perpetuity. We haven't seen ourselves as having a purpose, let alone one focused on contribution to the world outside of ourselves or our own families.

> If the highest level we can attain is community actualization, what can you do now to give (and receive) more healing and love in the world?

## Untended Fields

Some will argue that self-healing and restoration of the earth have nothing to do with business or organizational leadership. I disagree. We have left both of these things largely untended, to the point of complete disconnection. So, clearly doing more of the same and expecting any different result is not the answer.

Our society has made homogeneity the goal, and when we walk around asleep, voiceless, or fixated, we miss the awe of this place. We continue to abuse the planet the same way we experienced trauma as children. All beings deserve better. And, as with trauma, just because it's not our fault doesn't mean it's not our responsibility. We have incredible tools at our disposal. Every leader has the innate ability to remember their reason for being here, and the wisdom to walk a different path; as I've said before, this comes down to courage and willingness.

So, People Pleasers, we need you to do the work and realize that your voice matters. We need you to stop shrinking at the thought of being seen for who you are, afraid that others will judge your differences the same way you have. In reality, your heart is as big as the universe—just like mine—and we need more loving leaders to be actively healing and on the right side of history.

People Controllers, the gift you have to get things done is needed now more than ever. An increase in self-awareness and compassion will allow us to collaborate and get further together. Your immediate responsibility is to unpack why you feel the need to have power over others. This is not who you are at the core. I know this is not who you would choose to be. We need you to remember who you are and why you incarnated at this time. We need you. Full stop.

And for those of you who might sit somewhere in between, we especially need you because you're the closest thing we have to the choir. Together, our voices can grow and attract others who are beginning to wake up. To build a healthy and honorable society, we need humans who are led by their hearts and conscience to reinvent our systems and transform mindsets. Now is the moment to uplift time-honored wisdom alongside astonishing scientific and technological advancements. We must act with integrity and connect to our profound inner wisdom, which perceives the wonder of existence even during chaos and confusion.

Ultimately, healing ourselves and our planet is not separate from business or leadership—it is the very purpose. When we reconnect with our True Nature, we realize our interconnectedness. Though the path forward requires courage, by uplifting wisdom and acting with integrity, we can collaborate to build a society that works for all. When we give to others, we receive the priceless gift of meaning. When we give, we receive the gift of belonging to something greater than ourselves. By remembering who we are, and why we are here, we can transform ourselves and our world.

# 24

## Project Rebuild

THERE ARE MANY reasons why Indigenous peoples refer to plants as the *strength of the earth*. They are intelligent and resilient and have so much to teach us. At the tail end of my Ayahuasca journey in Peru, I had the honor of witnessing the reciprocal reverence that is possible for us all. The final vignette that I was shown enabled me to understand where we might be headed as a global ecosystem first, and as humanity second.

Soaring slowly below cloud level, I could see a return to symbiosis. As opposed to *natural resources* being available as raw materials, property, or capital to humans, we were in intimate relationship with nature. We worked with the breathtaking biodiversity and topography instead of going against natural law for the benefit of our singular species. We abided by gratitude-centricity, and we knew the land as a library, as medicine, and as a source of wonderment. Humans worked together seamlessly, bartered goods, and combined their innate gifts and technical prowess in the most innovative ways imaginable. There were groups and leaders of groups, of course, yet the latter changed based on what needed to be accomplished. Now, there were also fewer people throughout this vision and I was privy to only one portion of the world, but I got the distinct sense that this was a microcosm of the new global systems of currency, food production, and business. Some of our current systems seemed unnecessary and were nowhere to

195

be found. To me, this version of our world felt like an unending exchange of unconditional love and respect for every being.

Sounds pretty incredible, doesn't it? Yes, I was under the influence of sacred plant medicine—what Western medicine renames as a *psychedelic*, meaning "manifesting the mind."[1] But this was no drug-induced delusion; it felt very much like a visual blueprint for the world I want to have a hand in rebuilding. Though the path requires persistence in the face of uncertainty, humanity is ready. Light is within reach if we dare to see that we are one.

This is about remembering who we are, the reverence we hold in our hearts for all our kin, the innate wisdom we possess, and the power we have to dismantle the corrupt, supremacist systems that work in opposition to our True Nature. The few who benefit from these systems do not represent the collective heart; they just happen to have the loudest voices at the moment. And raised voices can be activating; anyone who has grown up in an environment where yelling and screaming were standard startles easily. Loud voices can make the most powerful of us back down without correlating why. That is the power and intricacy of trauma and leadership; it can keep some in a constant state of voicelessness and others so inflamed that projection is mistaken for safety.

Some of us are awakening, and some are already wide-eyed and ready to go. Just because the most vocal among the dominant group are afraid of what will happen when they lose their foothold doesn't mean that any more of us need to stay quiet or shrink. In fact, our voices and actions are needed now more than ever. Christian nationalists and those who hold many of their same ideologies—perhaps including some of your own neighbors and family members—as well as extremists around the globe are attempting to force a very different world into existence than most of us envision. This feels like the one place where we do need to take a stand on one side or the other—one of the few places where I take no issue with the existence of a binary. One world seems arid, where homogeneity reigns supreme, monoculture and fossil fuels continue to destroy our home, and there are ever-tightening restrictions on our bodies and the extent to which we can be free. The other world feels lush, kind, and generative, where business can be conducted with respect, human ingenuity can ensure the perpetuation of all species, and we can all express the wholeness of who we are.

As leaders, we can choose to move people through an existing system, or advocate for a few minor revisions, knowing full well that an overhaul is on the horizon. I think a few on the political right, most in the middle, and nearly all left-wingers can agree that the systems in which we live are broken. Not irreparably damaged, but certainly in need of a rebuild. Part of the reason we need to heal to lead is to create a collective buffer against authoritarianism. When we focus on repairing the systems that are harmful—because they were designed to extract, produce, and disproportionately benefit 1% of the population above all else—we begin to use our own healing for the benefit of others. Much like I've shared my story in this book and methods of experiential healing with you online at **MyHealingMenu.com**, we help others awaken to the ceilinglessness of themselves. We inspire new ways of thinking, feeling, and giving. When we act as the way-showers of reciprocity, we become part of a generative ecosystem. Though we have not seen that modeled at scale, many among us have brilliant ideas about how to return and many others are already showing us the way on local levels. To remember, we need each other.

As Gina Hayden eloquently reminds us, "the opposite of fear is love. This shows up in us as a deep and abiding trust in life. The trust prompts the conscious leader to move away from trying to control things with [their] mind towards listening quietly, inwardly, to what wants to emerge next. The conscious leader looks for the role [they] can play in the process of life. 'Me' to 'we' is not an act of mind but an act of heart, marked by the surrender of our own egoic will in favor of being part of all of life and the generative acts that support it."[2]

## The Runway to Freedom

I'd like to leave you with the story of an exemplary, high-conscious leader who is just like you and me. Her story is unique, and we can all relate to portions of it—especially how the trauma she experienced as a child impacted her leadership style.

Kristine Deer was the CEO and founder of K-DEER, an activewear brand that started in her childhood bedroom after a 2009 recession layoff. She had turned to hot yoga, which led to resourcefully making the clothing she couldn't find to meet the demands of the daily practice. Over her 12-year tenure, Kristine was committed to ensuring that the brand's carbon footprint was as low as possible, knitting, printing, and manufacturing within a 150-mile radius of the company's headquarters in New Jersey. Pandemic-related supply chain disruption—and a commitment to high quality and process transparency—ultimately forced her to close in 2022. For Kristine, it was more important to stay in integrity than to stay in business.

K-DEER was also the antithesis of fast fashion, and many customers still boast about the quality of their apparel after years of wear. The sale of her Signature Stripe Collection translated into social impact to the tune of a quarter of a million dollars donated to local and national charities. Beyond all of this, the brand drew a community of kindred spirits from all over the world who shared the values of kindness, inclusion, self-expression, and well-being. K-DEER was sold in yoga studios, department stores, and fitness boutiques across the world, was and continues to be worn by celebrities, and as with most successful designers, was knocked off by several well-known activewear brands.

When Kristine was just 11 years old, her dad, Jean, had a massive stroke. The brain injury led to right-body paralysis and severe global aphasia, which meant that although his intelligence and cognitive abilities remained fully intact, he was unable to process and use language. Along with her mother and two sisters, Kristine became a caregiver to her father from a young age. About the correlation between her leadership and healing journey, she recounts:

> I cannot recall being told that my dad's communication disorder was permanent or that his inability to speak was called *aphasia*. Empathetic to my mom's experience of this life-changing event, I efforted at being good and not causing her any more stress. In retrospect, I can see this is the origin of my perfectionism, hypervigilance, and people-pleasing tendencies. During those formative years, I hid the majority of my self-expression to avoid judgment, rejection, and abandonment from my family and peers. By my early teens, I was an expert at emotional suppression, which I now know was also the likely birthplace of depression.

My dad's care schedule subconsciously conditioned me to put everyone's needs before my own from a very young age. Rarely asking for help as a family carried over into my business, perpetuating a cycle of burnout, decision fatigue, and loneliness. Employees walked on eggshells because my depression, exhaustion, and unprocessed trauma caused me to be reactive, avoidant, and emotive. In early 2018, something had to give. I was checked out, stuck, and required more medication to function. I came out publicly about my depression, which felt really vulnerable because I feared being seen as unreliable or untrustworthy. Revealing that huge secret gave me the courage to come out as gay at 35, early on in the pandemic. I learned that when you shine a light on the parts you have hidden, you give them permission to be seen and set free. Naming my dad's stroke as childhood trauma and the origin of my mental health challenges, and then naming my sexual identity, allowed me to remove the masks I had worn for so long.

Since my dad's passing at the end of 2022—my family, his beloved aide Anny, Kelly, and me by his side—grief has provided a lot of growth. Grieving the loss of my dad, my role in my family, my business, and the life I thought I was expected to live, is helping reveal the gap between who I thought I was and the true Self I am continuing to discover. The work of healing makes all the difference in becoming a high-conscious leader. Being honest about where I slip out of integrity and into my trauma responses is my responsibility. Nowadays, I'm less concerned about corporate strengths and weaknesses and more focused on what requires more healing, rest, love, and compassion. Looking back, I was so hard on myself, operating from fear and ego, holding myself back from honest self-expression, and unconsciously discouraging opportunities from coming into my life. Utilizing therapy, core energetics, ketamine, and other trauma integration modalities, I am becoming whole again. After so much loss and a newfound commitment to inner healing work, I feel prepared and inspired to expand my impact in the next chapter of K-DEER.[3]

I am intimately familiar with Kristine's story because I have had a front-row seat since she closed the first iteration of her business.

Kristine is my partner in life, and I have had the absolute honor of loving this human alongside her loss, grief, healing, self-discovery—and how she lights the way for others to shine wherever she goes. One of the most beautiful parts of my own journey in the last couple of years has been witnessing the intentionality and trust that are at the foundation of her innate leadership. Recently, Kristine was trained as a trauma-informed coach as well, with plans to apply that knowledge to her next conscious venture. She is actively grieving, committed to healing, and aware that her self-work is making an intergenerational and global impact.

## The Revolution Is Already Here

Know that this, too, is the antithesis of an ending. Because you've finished this book, more honest conversations can now begin. Regardless of who you were when you began reading, I want to thank you for recognizing the moral imperative that is your own posttraumatic growth. Your commitment to healing, and the nonlinear path you will follow, is entirely up to you. The journey of trauma healing spirals upward, full of challenges, setbacks, and breakthroughs. Yet with perseverance, compassion, and the support of others, real transformation is more than possible. By facing our inner wounds, we liberate not only ourselves but also those around us. By daring to be vulnerable, leaning into discomfort, and modeling authenticity, we pave the way for others to find wholeness. The culture we cultivate through our example has the power to heal or harm; may we have the wisdom and courage to choose healing, again and again.

I cannot foresee how your particular journey will unfold, what modalities you'll use, or how long it might take for you to realize that your own revolution is in progress. What I can guarantee is impact. Integrating your trauma will change you. The people under your care will experience the difference in your leadership style, and you will find yourself invested in the success of strangers who soon become sacred.

This is the revolution—one heart, one leader, one organization at a time. We will all find each other, and the pockets of people everywhere doing their work will converge. The old paradigms of leadership through control and coercion are giving way to models rooted in self-empowerment and reciprocity. There are no quick fixes or easy answers, but when we stay the course together, we will meet the new day—a day when all people can bring their whole, healed selves to solve the challenges ahead. The road is long, yet we are far from alone. We will walk it with brave hearts, hand in hand, until every wound is healed, and every soul is free.

# Notes

## Prologue

1. Science Reference Section, Library of Congress. "Why Do Geese Fly in a V?" Everyday Mysteries: Fun Science Facts from the Library of Congress, November 19, 2019; accessed July 28, 2023: https://www.loc.gov/everyday-mysteries/zoology/item/why-do-geese-fly-in-a-v/
2. Kimmerer, Robin Wall. "Skywoman Falling," *Braiding Sweetgrass: Indigenous Wisdom, Scientific Knowledge, and the Teachings of Plants.* Minneapolis: Milkweed Editions, 2013, pp. 3–10.

## Introduction

1. Brown, Brené. *Dare to Lead: Brave Work. Tough Conversations. Whole Hearts.* New York: Random House Publishing Group, 2018, p. 4.
2. Kornfield, Jack. *The Art of Forgiveness, Lovingkindness, and Peace.* New York: Bantam Books, 2002, p. 54. Copyright © 2002 by Jack Kornfield. Used by permission of Bantam Books, an imprint of Random House, a division of Penguin Random House LLC. All rights reserved.
3. Pacia, Danielle M. "Reproductive Rights vs. Reproductive Justice: Why the Difference Matters in Bioethics" *Bill of Health*, the blog of the Petrie-Flom Center at Harvard Law School, November 3, 2020; accessed December 17, 2023: https://blog.petrieflom.law.harvard.edu/2020/11/03/reproductive-rights-justice-bioethics/

## Part I: Kintsukuroi

1. Jalāl al-Dīn Rūmī. *Selected Poems.* New York: Penguin Books, 2004, p. 142.

## Chapter 1: Why We Become Leaders

1. Bilyue, Tom. "Gabor Maté on How We Become Who We Are," Impact Theory podcast, 2021: https://www.youtube.com/watch?v=c2cJb1QeMIQ
2. *The Wisdom of Trauma*, featuring Dr. Gabor Maté, directed by Maurizio and Zaya Benazzo. Sebastopol, CA: Science and Nonduality, 2021: https://thewisdomoftrauma.com.
3. Blume, E. Sue. *Secret Survivors: Uncovering Incest and Its Aftereffects in Women.* New York: Random House Publishing Group, 1998, p. 246.
4. Chamine, Shirzad. Positive Intelligence website: https://support .positiveintelligence.com/article/116-stickler
5. Kraft, Dave. *Mistakes Leaders Make Wheaton, IL,* p. 110. Copyright © 2012. Used by permission of Crossway, a publishing ministry of Good News Publishers, Wheaton, IL 60187: www.crossway.org.
6. Chestnut, Beatrice. *The 9 Types of Leadership: Mastering the Art of People in the 21st Century Workplace.* Brentwood, TN: Post Hill Press, 2017.
7. Chamine, Positive Intelligence website: https://support.positiveintelligence .com/article/114-pleaser

## Chapter 2: Low-Conscious Leaders Are Everywhere

1. Dethmer, Jim, Diana Chapman, and Kaley Klemp. *The 15 Commitments of Conscious Leadership: A New Paradigm for Sustainable Success.* Scott Valley, CA: Conscious Leadership Group, 2015, p. 23
2. van der Kolk, Bessel. *The Body Keeps the Score: Brain, Mind, and Body in the Healing of Trauma.* New York: Penguin Publishing Group, 2015, p. 3. Excerpts used by permission of Viking Books, an imprint of Penguin Publishing Group, a division of Penguin Random House LLC. All rights reserved.
3. Ibid.
4. Ibid.
5. Hayden, Gina. *Becoming a Conscious Leader: How to Lead Successfully in a World That's Waking Up.* Devon, UK: Write Factor, 2016, p. 121.
6. Ibid.

7. Friedman, Lisa. "Biden Administration Approves Huge Alaska Oil Project," *New York Times*, March 12, 2023: https://www.nytimes.com /2023/03/12/climate/biden-willow-arctic-drilling-restrictions.html

8. Bustillo, Ximena. "Biden Ends Drilling in ANWR, Sparking Criticism, as Willow Project Moves Forward," National Public Radio, September 6, 2023, updated September 7, 2023: https://www.npr .org/2023/09/06/1197945859/anwr-alaska-drilling-oil-gas-leases -environment-energy-climate-change

9. Sweney, Mark, and Matthew Taylor. "UK Go-ahead for North Sea Oil and Gas Field Angers Environmental Groups," *Guardian*, September 27, 2023: https://www.theguardian.com/business/2023/sep/27/uk-gives -go-ahead-to-develop-rosebank-oil-and-gas-field-in-north-sea

10. Faguy, Ana. "DeSantis Signs Bill Banning Public Colleges from Funding Diversity Programs," *Forbes*, May 15, 2023: https://www.forbes.com /sites/anafaguy/2023/05/15/desantis-signs-bill-banning-public-colleges -from-funding-diversity-programs/?sh=2acf44b31d80

11. Chamorro-Premuzic, Tomas. "Why Do So Many Incompetent Men Become Leaders?" *Harvard Business Review*, August 22, 2013: https:// hbr.org/2013/08/why-do-so-many-incompetent-men

12. Grace, Miriam. "Origins of Leadership: The Etymology of Leadership," International Leadership Association conference, November 6–8, 2003, p. 3: https://ilaglobalnetwork.org/mgrace/

13. Kiger, Patrick. "7 Negative Effects of the Industrial Revolution," History .com, A&E Television Networks LLC, November 9, 2021: https://www .history.com/news/industrial-revolution-negative-effects

14. Frances Willard House Museum. "19th Century Reform Movements," Truth-Telling: Frances Willard and Ida B. Wells website: https://scalar .usc.edu/works/willard-and-wells/19th-century-reform-movements

15. Northouse, Peter. *Leadership: Theory and Practice.* London: SAGE Publications, 2015, p. 2.

16. King, Michelle. "The 1950s Leadership Ideal Won't Serve Us in 2030," Recruiter.com: https://www.recruiter.com/recruiting/the-1950s -leadership-ideal-wont-serve-us-in-2030/

17. Foster, Justin. Personal communication with the author, April 21, 2023.

18. Oyserman, Daphna, et al. "When Mothers Have Serious Mental Health Problems: Parenting as a Proximal Mediator," *Journal of Adolescence* 28 (2005): 443–463.

19. Van der Kolk, *The Body Keeps the Score*, p. 102.

## Chapter 3: The Wound in the Room

1. Maté, Gabor. "Mental Illness and Adaptation," Leading Edge Seminars webinar; accessed January 7, 2022: https://leadingedgeseminars.org /event/mental-illness-or-adaptation-how-to-help-challenging-clients/
2. Slater, Kevin Michael. Personal communication with the author, March 8, 2023.
3. Boring, Brandon, et al. "Over-Rating Pain Is Overrated: A Fundamental Self-Other Bias in Pain Reporting Behavior," *Journal of Pain* 23, no. 10 (October 2022): p. 1780.
4. Ibid, p. 1785.
5. Boyes, Alice. "4 Ways to Destigmatize Mental Health at Work," *Forbes*, August 31, 2020: https://www.forbes.com/sites/aliceboyes/2020/08/31/4 -ways-to-destigmatize-mental-health-at-work/?sh=71349076e49d
6. Mills, Wendy. "Survivor Leaders: A Grounded Theory Inquiry into Leadership Practices of Childhood Trauma Survivors," PhD diss., University of Missouri-Columbia, 2010.
7. Ibid.
8. Ibid.
9. Ibid.
10. Ibid.
11. Mills, Wendy. Personal communication with the author, January 7, 2022.

## Chapter 4: Why Now?

1. Rosen, Bob, and Emma Kate Swann. "Grounded and Conscious: The New Leadership Imperative," SHRM Executive Network, *People + Strategy Journal*, Fall 2018; accessed August 10, 2023: https://www .shrm.org/executive/resources/people-strategy-journal/fall-2018/pages /grounded-conscious.aspx
2. Franck, Thomas. "SEC Approves Nasdaq's Plan to Boost Diversity on Corporate Boards," CNBC.com, August 6, 2021: https://www.cnbc .com/2021/08/06/sec-approves-nasdaqs-plan-to-boost-diversity-on -corporate-boards.html
3. Dixon-Fyle, Sundiatu, et al. "Diversity Wins: How Inclusion Matters," McKinsey & Company, May 19, 2020: https://www.mckinsey.com/featured -insights/diversity-and-inclusion/diversity-wins-how-inclusion-matters
4. Napikoski, Linda. "Patriarchal Society According to Feminism," ThoughtCo., February 11, 2021: thoughtco.com/patriarchal-society -feminism-definition-3528978.

5. Vaid-Menon, Alok. "Alok Vaid-Menon: The Urgent Need for Compassion," Man Enough Podcast, July 26, 2021: https://manenough.com/alok/; Courtesy of Wayfarer Studios LLC.

6. Ely, Robin, and David Thomas. "Getting Serious About Diversity: Enough Already with the Business Case," *Harvard Business Review*, November–December 2020; accessed July 9, 2023: https://hbr.org/2020/11/getting-serious-about-diversity-enough-already-with-the-business-case

7. Hayden, Gina. *Becoming a Conscious Leader: How to Lead Successfully in a World That's Waking Up*. Devon, UK: Write Factor, 2016, p. 87.

8. US Environmental Protection Agency. "Impacts of Climate Change," last updated December 30, 2022: https://www.epa.gov/climatechangescience/impacts-climate-change

9. United Nations General Assembly. "Transforming Our World: The 2030 Agenda for Sustainable Development," United Nations, October 21, 2015: https://sdgs.un.org/2030agenda

10. Associated Press. "Judge Sides with Young Activists in First-of-Its-Kind Climate Change Trial in Montana," National Public Radio, August 14, 2023: https://www.npr.org/2023/08/14/1193780700/montana-climate-change-trial-ruling

## Part II: Preparing for the Journey

1. Brown, Barrett. "The Future of Leadership for Conscious Capitalism," MetaIntegral Associates, 2013, p.13: https://www.academia.edu/6605006/The_Future_of_Leadership_for_Conscious_Capitalism

## Chapter 5: Contextualizing Trauma

1. Grande, Mari. "Understanding the Mother Wound: Signs, Symptoms, and Treatment of Maternal Trauma," LinkedIn, March 10, 2022: https://www.linkedin.com/pulse/understanding-mother-wound-signs-symptoms-treatment-mari/

2. Webster, Bethany. *Discovering the Inner Mother: A Guide to Healing the Mother Wound and Claiming Your Personal Power*. New York: HarperCollins Publishers, 2021, p. 7.

3. Maté, Gabor. *The Wisdom of Trauma*, featuring Dr. Gabor Maté, directed by Maurizio and Zaya Benazzo. Sebastopol, CA: Science and Nonduality, 2021: https://thewisdomoftrauma.com.

4. Centers for Disease Control and Prevention. "Fast Facts: Preventing Adverse Childhood Experiences," US Department of Health and Human Services. Page last reviewed April 6, 2022: https://www.cdc .gov/violenceprevention/aces/fastfact.html

5. Prevent Child Abuse America. "Adverse Childhood Experiences (ACEs) One-Pager," 2021, p. 2: https://preventchildabuse.org/wpcontent /uploads/2021/12/PCA-Aces-One-Pager-2021-10202021.pdf

6. Sareen, Jitender, Murray Stine, and Michael Friedman. "Posttraumatic Stress Disorder in Adults: Epidemiology, Pathophysiology, Clinical Manifestations, Course Assessment, and Diagnosis," Wolters Kluwer Medknow Publications, UpToDate reprint 2023: https://www.uptodate .com/contents/posttraumatic-stress-disorder-in-adults-epidemiology -pathophysiology-clinical-manifestations-course-assessment-and -diagnosis/print

7. PTSD Alliance. "Post Traumatic Stress Disorder Fact Sheet," Sidran Institute, 2018, p. 1: https://www.sidran.org/wp-content/uploads/2018 /11/Post-Traumatic-Stress-Disorder-Fact-Sheet-.pdf

8. Barbash, Elyssa. "Different Types of Trauma: Small 't' Versus Large 'T,'" *Psychology Today*, March 13, 2017: https://www.psychologytoday .com/us/blog/trauma-and-hope/201703/different-types-trauma-small-t -versus-large-t

9. Campbell, Kelly. "Trauma and Entrepreneurship, with Nicole Lewis-Keeber," THRIVE podcast, Ep. 142, February 21, 2023: https://www .youtube.com/watch?v=RbTWllqsAME

10. Foundation Trust. "Systemic Trauma," *Complex Trauma Resources*, 2023. https://www.complextrauma.org/glossary/systemic-trauma/

11. Bhui, Kamaldeep, et al. "Perceptions of Work Stress Causes and Effective Interventions in Employees Working in Public, Private and Non-Governmental Organisations: A Qualitative Study." *BJPsych Bulletin* 40, no. 6 (2016): 318–325.

12. Sams, Rachel. "Call It What It Is: Organizational Trauma Isn't Burnout," *Risk eNews*, Nonprofit Risk Management Center, February 16, 2022: https://nonprofitrisk.org/resources/e-news/call-it-what-it-is -organizational-trauma-isnt-burnout/

13. Vivian, Pat, and Shana Hormann. *Organizational Trauma and Healing*. Scotts Valley, CA: CreateSpace Independent Publishing Platform, 2013.

14. Administration for Children and Families, "Secondary Traumatic Stress," US Department of Health and Human Services: https://www .acf.hhs.gov/trauma-toolkit/secondary-traumatic-stress

15. Hirschberger, Gilad. "Collective Trauma and the Social Construction of Meaning," *Frontiers in Psychology* 9 (August 10, 2018): 1441.

16. Cuncic, Arlin. "What Does It Mean to Be 'Triggered'? Types of Triggering Events and Coping Strategies," Verywell Mind, December 3, 2020: https://www.verywellmind.com/what-does-it-mean-to-be-triggered-4175432

17. Groves, Mark. "Triggers are invitations to pay attention." Instagram, @createthelove, January 20, 2022: https://www.instagram.com/reel/CZDQW24I1Ps/

18. Walker, Pete. "The 4Fs: A Trauma Typology in Complex PTSD," 2009: http://www.pete-walker.com/fourFs_TraumaTypologyComplexPTSD.htm

19. Ibid.

20. Ibid.

21. Ibid.

22. Buckholtz, Joshua, and Andreas Meyer-Lindenberg, "Psychopathology and the Human Connectome: Toward a Transdiagnostic Model of Risk for Mental Illness," *Neuron* 74, no. 6 (2012): 990–1004.

23. Walker, "The 4Fs."

24. van der Kolk, Bessel. *The Body Keeps the Score: Brain, Mind, and Body in the Healing of Trauma.* New York: Penguin Publishing Group, 2015, p. 54.

25. Krippner, Stanley, and Deirdre Barrett. "Transgenerational Trauma." *Journal of Mind and Behavior* 40, no. 1 (2019): 53–62.

26. Bierer, Linda, et al. "Intergenerational Effects of Maternal Holocaust Exposure on FKBP5 Methylation," *American Journal of Psychiatry* 177, no. 8 (2020): 744–753.

27. Davidson, Sol, and Paul Brown. From a late-stage draft of a paper on childhood trauma and neuropolitics (2023) to be published. Courtesy of Davidson and Brown.

28. In the draft of their paper shared with the author, Davidson and Brown cite the following sources in support of their insights regarding the early life trauma of these public figures: Jane Allen Stevens, "How Vladimir Putin's Childhood Is Affecting Us All," ACES Too High News, March 2, 2022: https://acestoohigh.com/2022/03/02/how-vladimir-putins-childhood-is-affecting-us-all/; Mary L. Trump, *Too Much and Never Enough: How My Family Created the World's Most Dangerous Man*, New York: Simon & Schuster, 2020; Christopher Titmus, "The Personality/Psychology of Boris Johnson. Does He Show Signs of Being Traumatised? Is He a Victim of Domestic Violence? An Analysis," Christopher Titmus

Dharma blog, February 21, 2022: https://www.christophertitmussblog
.org/the-personality-psychology-of-boris-johnson-does-he-show-signs
-of-being-traumatised-is-he-a-victim-of-domestic-violence-an-analysis;
National Public Radio, "'Hidden History' of Koch Brothers Traces Their
Childhood and Political Rise," Fresh Air, January 19, 2016: https://
www.npr.org/2016/01/19/463565987/hidden-history-of-koch-brothers
-traces-their-childhood-and-political-rise; Wikipedia contributors,
"Early Life of Joseph Stalin," Wikipedia, accessed September 28, 2023:
https://en.wikipedia.org/w/index.php?title=Early_life_of_Joseph
_Stalin&oldid=1175076586; Alice Miller, "Hitler's Childhood: From
Hidden to Manifest Horror," in Miller's For Your Own Good: Hidden
Cruelty in Child-Rearing and the Roots of Violence. New York: Farrar,
Straus and Giroux, 1990; and Melissa Stevens, "Elon Musk's Early Life:
From Childhood to College," Shortform, April 3, 2022: https://www
.shortform.com/blog/elon-musk-early-life.

29. Hoskinson, Steve A. "A New Threshold: Trauma Means Unintegrated
Resource." Organic Intelligence blog, 2015. https://organicintelligence
.org/

30. Mouer, Monica. "Healing the Child Within: Integrating to Become
Whole," Center for Family Transformation blog, August 17, 2020:
https://www.familytransformation.com/2020/08/17/healing-the-child
-within-integrating-to-become-whole/

31. Menakem, Resmaa. My Grandmother's Hands: Racialized Trauma and the
Pathway to Mending Our Hearts and Bodies. Las Vegas: Central Recovery
Press, 2017, p. 12.

## Chapter 6: Maintenance Versus Healing

1. Wahass, Saeed. "The Role of Psychologists in Health Care Delivery,"
Journal of Family & Community Medicine 12, no. 2 (2005): 63–70.

2. CBT Clinic. "Pros and Cons of CBT Therapy," Riverside Natural Health
Centre: http://www.thecbtclinic.com/pros-cons-of-cbt-therapy

3. See, for example, Gillas, George. "Time Line Therapy Overview,"
YouTube, June 17, 2014; accessed July 28, 2023: https://www.youtube
.com/watch?v=Fv3C-aweGl4

4. CBT Clinic. "Pros and Cons of CBT Therapy."

5. van der Kolk, Bessel. The Body Keeps the Score: Brain, Mind, and
Body in the Healing of Trauma. New York: Penguin Publishing Group,
2015, p. 47.

6. Fossella, Tina. "Human Nature, Buddha Nature: On Spiritual Bypassing, Relationship, and the Dharma—An Interview with John Welwood," Johnwelwood.com, 2011, p. 1: http://www.johnwelwood.com/articles /TRIC_interview_uncut.pdf

7. Brown, Lachlan. "The Real Meaning of Buddhist Detachment and Why Most of Us Get It Wrong," HackSpirit, October 14, 2022: https:// hackspirit.com/zen-master-explains-real-meaning-non-attachment -us-get-wrong/

8. Amelia V. Gallucci-Cirio Library. "Anti-Racism Resources: Racial Colorblindness," Fitchburg State University, last updated March 15, 2023: https://fitchburgstate.libguides.com/c.php?g=1046516&p=7616506

9. Quintero, Samara, and Jamie Long. "Toxic Positivity: The Dark Side of Positive Vibes," Psychology Group, Fort Lauderdale: https:// thepsychologygroup.com/toxic-positivity/

10. Ibid.

11. Resilience Institute. "Are There Downsides to Resilience?" Resilience Institute blog, March 12, 2023: https://resiliencei.com/blog/are-there -downsides-to-resilience

12. Ibid.

13. Oroszi, Tamás, et al. "Vibration Detection: Its Function and Recent Advances in Medical Applications." *F1000Research* 9 F1000 Faculty Rev-619, June 17, 2020: https://www.ncbi.nlm.nih.gov/pmc/articles /PMC7308885/

14. Rose, Brian. "The Vibrational Frequencies of the Human Body," 2021: https://www.researchgate.net/publication/354326235_The_Vibrational _Frequencies_of_the_Human_Body

15. Newport Institute. "Is Manifestation Bad for Mental Health?" January 27, 2023: https://www.newportinstitute.com/resources/mental-health /manifesting-change/

16. Renzi, Melissa. "Spiritual Bypass: 5 Common Examples, Why It Happens, and What to Do," Melissanoelrenzi.com, July 23, 2020: https:// melissanoelrenzi.com/spiritual-bypass/

17. Rabbi Ridberg, Yael. "Sin and Forgiveness," Reconstructing Judaism website, August 8, 2016: https://www.reconstructingjudaism.org/article /sin-and-forgiveness/

18. Chattopadhyay, Madhumita. "Sin (Buddhism)," In K.T.S. Sarao and J. D. Long (eds.), "Buddhism and Jainism," *Encyclopedia of Indian Religions*. Dordrecht: Springer, 2017; accessed April 13, 2023: https://link.springer .com/referenceworkentry/10.1007/978-94-024-0852-2_354

## Chapter 7: What Is High-Conscious Leadership?

1. Gelb, Michael, and Raj Sisodia. "How to Become a Healing Leader," interview by Skip Prichard, Leadership Insights blog, October 14, 2019: https://www.skipprichard.com/how-to-become-a-healing-leader/
2. Dethmer, Jim, Diana Chapman, and Kaley Klemp. *The 15 Commitments of Conscious Leadership: A New Paradigm for Sustainable Success*. Scott Valley, CA: Conscious Leadership Group, 2015, p. 14.
3. Janni, Nicholas. *Leader as Healer: A New Paradigm for 21st-Century Leadership*. London: LID Publishing, 2022.
4. See Reiki Association. "Usui Shiki Ryoho: The Usui System of Reiki Healing," Reikiassociation.net; accessed August 26, 2024: https://www.reikiassociation.net/usui-shiki-ryoho
5. Early, Gene. "Elevating Leadership: Leader as Healer," LinkedIn, November 13, 2020: https://www.linkedin.com/pulse/elevating-leadership-leader-healer-gene-early-phd/

## Chapter 8: Four Fundamentals

1. Von Sturmer, Lucy. "SB'19 Paris: The Future of Leadership Is Bold, Brave and Feminine," Sustainable Brands, April 25, 2019: https://sustainablebrands.com/read/leadership/sb-19-paris-the-future-of-leadership-is-bold-brave-and-feminine
2. Livne-Tarandach, Reut, et al. "Cultivating Organizations as Healing Spaces: A Typology for Responding to Suffering and Advancing Social Justice," *Humanistic Management Journal*, 6 (2021): 373–404: https://link.springer.com/article/10.1007/s41463-021-00112-2
3. DuBose, Jennifer, et al. "Exploring the Concept of Healing Spaces," *Health Environments Research & Design Journal* 11 (1): 43–56, 2018.
4. Powley, Edward. "The Process and Mechanisms of Organizational Healing," *Journal of Applied Behavioral Science* 49, no. 1 (2013): 42–68.
5. Sarkar, Christian. "'The Healing Organization': An Interview with Raj Sisodia," *Marketing Journal*, November 3, 2019: https://www.marketingjournal.org/the-healing-organization-an-interview-with-raj-sisodia/
6. Winter, Larissa. "Organizational Trauma: A Phenomenological Study of Psychological Organizational Trauma and Its Effect on Employees and Organization," *Management* 14, no. 2 (2019): 122.
7. Powley, "Process and Mechanisms."
8. Winter, "Organizational Trauma," p. 120.

# Part III: When the Past Is Present

1. Myss, Caroline quoted in Schmidt, Barb. *The Practice: Simple Tools for Managing Stress, Finding Inner Peace, and Uncovering Happiness.* Deerfield Beach, FL: Health Communications, Inc., 2014, p. 61.

# Chapter 9: Fundamental #1: Integrating Trauma

1. van der Kolk, Bessel. *The Body Keeps the Score: Brain, Mind, and Body in the Healing of Trauma.* New York: Penguin Publishing Group, 2015, p. 97.
2. Davis, Laura. *Allies in Healing: When the Person You Love Is a Survivor of Child Sexual Abuse.* New York: HarperCollins, 2012, p. 29.
3. Gertel Kraybill, Odelya. "Roadmap After Trauma: Six Stages to Trauma Integration," *Psychology Today*, September 28, 2018: https://www.psychologytoday.com/us/blog/expressive-trauma-integration/201809/roadmap-after-trauma-six-stages-trauma-integration
4. Maté, Gabor, and Daniel Maté. *The Myth of Normal: Trauma, Illness, and Healing in a Toxic Culture.* New York: Penguin Publishing Group, 2022, p. 374.
5. Tull, Matthew. "Acceptance and Commitment Therapy (ACT) for PTSD," Verywell Mind, December 21, 2020: https://www.verywellmind.com/using-act-for-ptsd-2797661#
6. Lovering, Nancy. "Healing from Childhood Trauma: The Roles of Neuroplasticity and EMDR," PsychCentral, May 9, 2022: https://psychcentral.com/ptsd/the-roles-neuroplasticity-and-emdr-play-in-healing-from-childhood-trauma#trauma-changes-the-brain
7. Danese, Andrea, and Anne-Laura van Harmelen. "The Hidden Wounds of Childhood Trauma," *European Journal of Psychotraumatology* 8, sup. 7, 1375840, 2017: https://doi.org/10.1080/20008198.2017.1375840
8. Lebow, Hilary. "6 Neuroplasticity Exercises for Anxiety Relief," PsychCentral, November 3, 2021: https://psychcentral.com/anxiety/how-to-train-your-brain-to-alleviate-anxiety#neuroplasticity-exercises
9. Lovering, "Healing from Childhood Trauma."
10. Silvia, P. J. "Self-Awareness and the Regulation of Emotional Intensity," *Self and Identity* 1 (2002): 3–10: https://libres.uncg.edu/ir/uncg/f/P_Silvia_Self-awareness_2002.pdf
11. MedlinePlus. "Is Temperament Determined by Genetics?" National Library of Medicine (US); last updated July 12, 2022; accessed June 2, 2023: https://medlineplus.gov/genetics/understanding/traits/temperament/

12. Brown University. "Childhood Adversity Causes Changes in Genetics," ScienceDaily, February 27, 2012; accessed June 2, 2023: https://www.sciencedaily.com/releases/2012/02/120227152729.htm

## Chapter 10: Practicing Introspection

1. Hayden, Gina. *Becoming a Conscious Leader: How to Lead Successfully in a World That's Waking Up*. Devon, UK: Write Factor, 2016, p. 145.
2. Deshmukh, Vinod. "Consciousness, Awareness, and Presence: A Neurobiological Perspective." *International Journal of Yoga* 15, no. 2, 2022: https://www.ncbi.nlm.nih.gov/pmc/articles/PMC9623886/
3. Bartholomew, Kim, and Leonard Horowitz. "Attachment Styles Among Young Adults: A Test of a Four-Category Model," *Journal of Personality and Social Psychology* 61, no. 2 (1991): 226–244.
4. Ibid.
5. Attachment Project. "Disorganized Attachment: Causes & Symptoms," MindOnly Pty Ltd., July 2, 2020, updated September 12, 2022: https://www.attachmentproject.com/blog/disorganized-attachment/

## Chapter 11: An Awakening

1. Brown, Brené. *The Gifts of Imperfection*. Center City, MN: Hazelden Publishing, 2010, p. 39.
2. Jung, C. G. *Collected Works of C. G. Jung, Volume 12: Psychology and Alchemy*. Oxford, UK: Princeton University Press, 1980, p. 99. Used with permission of Princeton University Press from the *Collected Works of C. G. Jung, Volume 12: Psychology and Alchemy*, C. G. Jung, copyright © 1980; permission conveyed through Copyright Clearance Center, Inc.
3. Myss, Caroline. *Why People Don't Heal and How They Can*. New York: Harmony Books, 1997, p. 15.

## Chapter 12: Doing the Work

1. Dethmer, Jim, Diana Chapman, and Kaley Klemp. *The 15 Commitments of Conscious Leadership: A New Paradigm for Sustainable Success*. Scott Valley, CA: Conscious Leadership Group, 2015, pp. 239–240.
2. van der Kolk, Bessel. *The Body Keeps the Score: Brain, Mind, and Body in the Healing of Trauma*. New York: Penguin Publishing Group, 2015, p. 99.

3. Maslow, Abraham. "A Theory of Human Motivation," *Psychological Review* 50, no. 4 (1943): 370.

4. McAllister, Jeremy. "Healing Complex Trauma, Part II: The Path to Integration," GoodTherapy blog, January 26, 2016: https://www.goodtherapy.org/blog/healing-complex-trauma-part-ii-path-to-integration-0126164

5. Callaway, J. C., and C. S. Grob. "Ayahuasca Preparations and Serotonin Reuptake Inhibitors: A Potential Combination for Severe Adverse Interactions," *Journal of Psychoactive Drugs* 30, no. 4 (1998): 367–369; accessed July 10, 2023: https://pubmed.ncbi.nlm.nih.gov/9924842/

6. Drigas, Athanasios, and Eleni Mitsea. "The Triangle of Spiritual Intelligence, Metacognition, and Consciousness," *International Journal of Recent Contributions from Engineering Science & IT* 8, no. 1 (2020): https://www.researchgate.net/publication/340299250_The_Triangle_of_Spiritual_Intelligence_Metacognition_and_Consciousness

7. Graham, O. J., G. R. Saucedo, and M. Politi. "Experiences of Listening to Icaros During Ayahuasca Ceremonies at Centro Takiwasi: An Interpretive Phenomenological Analysis," *Anthropology of Consciousness*, 34: 35–67, 2023, p. 42; accessed July 11, 2023: https://anthrosource.onlinelibrary.wiley.com/doi/full/10.1111/anoc.12170

8. Greenspan, Miriam. *Healing Through the Dark Emotions: The Wisdom of Grief, Fear, and Despair.* Boulder, CO: Shambhala Publications, 2003, p. 257. Copyright © 2003 by Miriam Greenspan. Reprinted by arrangement with The Permissions Company LLC on behalf of Shambhala Publications, Inc., Boulder, Colorado, shambhala.com.

9. Gertel Kraybill, Odelya. "Roadmap After Trauma: Six Stages to Trauma Integration," *Psychology Today*, September 28, 2018: https://www.psychologytoday.com/us/blog/expressive-trauma-integration/201809/roadmap-after-trauma-six-stages-trauma-integration

10. Mouer, Monica. "Healing the Child Within: Integrating to Become Whole," Center for Family Transformation blog, August 17, 2020: https://www.familytransformation.com/2020/08/17/healing-the-child-within-integrating-to-become-whole/

## Part IV: True Strength

1. Godin, Seth. *Tribes: We Need You to Lead Us.* New York: Penguin Publishing Group, 2008, p. 55, copyright © 2008 by Do You Zoom, Inc. Used by permission of Portfolio, an imprint of Penguin Publishing Group, a division of Penguin Random House LLC. All rights reserved.

## Chapter 13: Fundamental #2: Embodying Vulnerability

1. Considine, Kevin. Personal communication with the author, December 31, 2020. Courtesy of Kevin Considine.
2. Omadeke, Janice. "The Best Leaders Aren't Afraid to Be Vulnerable," *Harvard Business Review*, July 2, 2022: https://hbr.org/2022/07/the-best -leaders-arent-afraid-of-being-vulnerable
3. Gaba, Sherry. "The Mother Wound: How Our Relationships with Our Mothers Effect Our Codependency," *Psychology Today*, October 25, 2019: https://www.psychologytoday.com/us/blog/addiction-and-recovery /201910/the-mother-wound

## Chapter 14: Failure's Great Gift

1. Fleischhauer, Monica, et al. "The Impostor Phenomenon: Toward a Better Understanding of the Nomological Network and Gender Differences," *Frontiers in Psychology* 12, November 17, 2021.
2. Clance, Pauline Rose, and Suzanne A. Imes. "The Impostor Phenomenon in High Achieving Women: Dynamics and Therapeutic Intervention," *Psychotherapy: Theory, Research & Practice* 15, no. 3 (1978): 241–247.
3. Goldhill, Olivia. "It Turns Out Men, Not Women, Suffer More from Imposter Syndrome," *Quartz*, June 9, 2018: https://qz.com/1296783/it -turns-out-men-not-women-suffer-more-from-imposter-syndrome
4. Clance, and Imes.
5. Tulshyan, Ruchika, and Jodi-Ann Burey, "Stop Telling Women They Have Imposter Syndrome," *Harvard Business Review*, February 11, 2021: https:// hbr.org/2021/02/stop-telling-women-they-have-imposter-syndrome
6. Ibid.
7. Rideout, Kira C. "Rainbow Impostors: Impostor Syndrome in the LGBTQ+ Community," bachelor's degree Capstone Project, California State University, Monterey Bay, 2021: https://digitalcommons.csumb.edu /caps_thes_all/1220
8. Owens, Alexandra. "What Is Imposter Syndrome?" Psycom, February 27, 2020, last updated December 22, 2021: https://www.psycom.net /imposter-syndrome
9. Hendricks, Gay. *The Big Leap: Conquer Your Hidden Fear and Take Life to the Next Level*. New York: HarperOne, 2009.

10. Hendricks, Gay. "Upper Limit Problem: The Only Problem We Need to Solve," SoulatPlay promotional video, March 3, 2022: https://www.youtube.com/watch?v=RaUOSKfddSc

## Chapter 15: The Value of Nothingness

1. Lewis-Keeber, Nicole. Personal communication with the author, June 1, 2023.
2. Ibid.
3. Koloroutis, Mary, and Michele Pole. "Trauma-Informed Leadership and Posttraumatic Growth," *Nursing Management* 52, no. 12 (2021): 28–34; accessed June 21, 2023: https://www.ncbi.nlm.nih.gov/pmc/articles/PMC8620727/
4. Tedeschi, Richard. "Growth After Trauma," *Harvard Business Review*, July–August 2020; accessed July 5, 2023: https://hbr.org/2020/07/growth-after-trauma

## Chapter 16: The Art of Implementation

1. Yazeed, Carey. "Black Women and Vulnerability: What Brené Brown Got Wrong," drcareyyazeed.com blog, April 5, 2023: https://drcareyyazeed.com/black-women-and-vulnerability-what-brene-brown-got-wrong/
2. Ward, Lindsay. "The Role of Vulnerability in Leadership: A Study to Understand How Vulnerability Contributes to Personal, Professional, and Organizational Success," LinkedIn, May 16, 2020: https://www.linkedin.com/pulse/role-vulnerability-leadership-study-understand-how-lindsay/
3. Ely, Robin, and David Thomas. "Getting Serious About Diversity: Enough Already with the Business Case," *Harvard Business Review*, November–December 2020; accessed July 9, 2023: https://hbr.org/2020/11/getting-serious-about-diversity-enough-already-with-the-business-case

## Part V: Care in Action

1. Goleman, Daniel. *Social Intelligence: The New Science of Human Relationships.* New York: Bantam Books, 2006, p. 54, copyright © 2006 by Daniel Goleman. Used by permission of Bantam Books, an imprint of Random House, a division of Penguin Random House LLC. All rights reserved.

## Chapter 17: Fundamental #3: Leading with Compassion

1. Goleman, Daniel. "Daniel Goleman and the Three Kinds of Empathy," SuperSoul Sunday, interview with Oprah Winfrey, March 20, 2016; accessed July 31, 2023: https://www.youtube.com/watch?v=q2KRS1WrhyE
2. Ibid.
3. Ibid.
4. Ventura, Michael. *Applied Empathy: The New Language of Leadership.* New York: Atria Books, 2019, p. 40.
5. Boyatzis, Richard, et al. "Examination of the Neural Substrates Activated in Memories of Experiences with Resonant and Dissonant Leaders," *Leadership Quarterly* 23, no. 2 (April 2012): 259–272.
6. Barsade, Sigal, and Olivia O'Neill. "What's Love Got to Do with It? A Longitudinal Study of the Culture of Companionate Love and Employee and Client Outcomes in a Long-term Care Setting," *Administrative Science Quarterly* 59 no. 4 (2014): 551–598.
7. Trzeciak, Stephen, Anthony Mazzarelli, and Emma Seppälä. "Leading with Compassion Has Research-Backed Benefits," *Harvard Business Review,* February 27, 2023: https://hbr.org/2023/02/leading-with-compassion-has-research-backed-benefits
8. Zoghbi-Manrique-de-Lara, Pablo, and Mercedes Viera-Armas. "Does Ethical Leadership Motivate Followers to Participate in Delivering Compassion?" *Journal of Business Ethics* 154 (2017): 195–210.
9. Tashjian, Sarah, et al. "Evidence from a Randomized Controlled Trial That Altruism Moderates the Effect of Prosocial Acts on Adolescent Well-Being." *Journal of Youth and Adolescence* 50, no. 1 (2021): 29–43.

## Chapter 18: Compassionate Intelligence

1. Armstrong, Martin. "Why Are Americans Quitting Their Jobs?" World Economic Forum, July 28, 2022: https://www.weforum.org/agenda/2022/07/quitting-jobs-reasons-workplace/
2. Bloom, Paul. "Think Empathy Makes the World a Better Place? Think Again. . ." *Observer,* February 18, 2017; accessed July 19, 2023: https://www.theguardian.com/commentisfree/2017/feb/19/think-empathy-makes-world-better-place-think-again
3. Koloroutis, Mary, and Michele Pole. "Trauma-Informed Leadership and Posttraumatic Growth," *Nursing Management* 52, no. 12 (2021): 28–34;

accessed August 9, 2023: https://www.ncbi.nlm.nih.gov/pmc/articles/PMC8620727/

4. Winder, Jessica. "The Difference Between HR and People Operations," LinkedIn, October 1, 2022; accessed July 22, 2023: https://www.linkedin.com/pulse/difference-between-hr-people-operations-shrl-cmhr-sphr-shrm-scp/

5. Ibid.

## Chapter 19: How We Respond Matters

1. Silberling, Amanda, and Alyssa Stringer. "Elon Musk's Twitter (now X): Everything You Need to Know, from Layoffs to Verification," *TechCrunch*, July 28, 2023: https://techcrunch.com/2023/07/28/elon-musk-twitter-everything-you-need-to-know/

2. Musk, Elon [@elonmusk]. "DEI Must DIE. The Point Was to End Discrimination, Not Replace It with Different Discrimination." December 15, 2023: https://twitter.com/elonmusk/status/1735568882499211557

3. Limb, Lottie. "Patagonia and Ecosia: The Big Companies Profiting the Earth Thanks to Eco-Conscious Founders," *EuroNews*, September 15, 2022; updated September 15, 2022: https://www.euronews.com/green/2022/09/15/billionaire-patagonia-boss-gives-company-away-to-fight-the-climate-crisis

4. Edleman, Richard, quoted in "Two-Thirds of Consumers Worldwide Now Buy on Beliefs," Edleman.com, October 2, 2018: https://www.edelman.com/news-awards/two-thirds-consumers-worldwide-now-buy-beliefs

## Chapter 20: A Shift in Intention

1. Beridze, Sesily. "'The Wisdom of the Wild': Nature's Guide to Eco-Leadership," Impakter.com, June 18, 2022; accessed August 12, 2023: https://impakter.com/eco-leadership-a-guide-sustainable-leadership-styles/

## Part VI: The Great Remembering

1. Viscott, David. *Finding Your Strength in Difficult Times: A Book of Meditations.* New York: McGraw-Hill, 1993, p. 87. Copyright © McGraw-Hill, all rights reserved. Reproduced with permission.

2. Scheele, Paul, and Masanori Kanda. "What Is Future Mapping?" Learning Strategies: https://www.learningstrategies.com/future-mapping/whatisit.asp

3. Lockwood, Patricia, et al. "Distinct Neural Representations for Prosocial and Self-Benefiting Effort," *Current Biology* 32, no. 19 (October 10, 2022): 4172–4185; accessed July 31, 2023: https://www.cell.com/current-biology/fulltext/S0960-9822(22)01287-8

## Chapter 22: Essential Work

1. United Nations. "Global Issues: Population," accessed August 30, 2023: https://www.un.org/en/global-issues/population

## Chapter 23: What We Receive When We Give

1. Kripalani, Simran, Basant Pradhan, and Kelly Gilrain. "The Potential Positive Epigenetic Effects of Various Mind-Body Therapies (MBTs): A Narrative Review," *Journal of Complementary and Integrative Medicine* 19, no. 4 (2022): 827–832.

2. Maslow, Abraham. "A Theory of Human Motivation," *Psychological Review* 50 (1943): 370–396.

3. Widhalm, Curt, and Katie Vernoy, "What Maslow Missed in His Hierarchy of Needs—The Native Self Actualization Model: An Interview with Dr. Sidney Stone Brown," Modern Therapist's Survival Guide podcast, August 8, 2022: https://therapyreimagined.com/modern-therapist-podcast/what-maslow-missed-in-his-hierarchy-of-needs-the-native-self-actualization-model-an-interview-with-dr-sidney-stone-brown/

4. Maslow, Abraham. *The Farther Reaches of Human Nature.* New York: Arkana/Penguin Books, 1971.

5. Ibid.

6. See Blackstock, Cindy. "The Emergence of the Breath of Life Theory," *Journal of Social Work Values and Ethics* 8, no. 1 (Spring 2011).

7. Widhalm and Vernoy, "What Maslow Missed."

8. Syed, Moin, and Fish, Jillian. "Revisiting Erik Erikson's Legacy on Culture, Race, and Ethnicity," *Identity: An International Journal of Theory and Research* 18 no. 4 (2018): 274–283.

9. Widhalm and Vernoy, "What Maslow Missed."

10. Jung, C. G. *Memories, Dreams, Reflections.* New York: Pantheon Books, 1973, p. 252.

# Chapter 24: Project Rebuild

1. See Celidwen, Yuria, et al. "Ethical Principles of Traditional Indigenous Medicine to Guide Western Psychedelic Research and Practice." *Lancet Regional Health Americas* 18 (December 16, 2022); accessed August 16, 2023: https://www.ncbi.nlm.nih.gov/pmc/articles/PMC9950658/
2. Hayden, Gina. *Becoming a Conscious Leader: How to Lead Successfully in a World That's Waking Up*. Devon, UK: Write Factor, 2016, p. 122.
3. Deer, Kristine. Personal communication with the author, October 29, 2023. Courtesy of Kristine Deer.

# Acknowledgments

To MY PARTNER, who is the embodiment of strength and kindness: Being in conscious partnership with you has unlocked the most profound expression of my heart.

To my family: Your unconditional love has made all the difference.

To my right hand and research lead: Our paths were destined to converge, and for that divinity, I am eternally grateful.

To the experts who contributed to this project: Thank you for your generosity and shared vision for a world full of healing leaders.

To my conscious-alpha counterpart and dear friend: Your constant, heart-led provocation helped me proudly get this project across the finish line.

To my content consultants along the way: Thank you for being certain that what I was writing was not my first book—and for asking the singular question that would guide me toward writing this one instead.

To my book proposal consultant: Your attention to detail and palpable encouragement every single step of the way has given me so much.

To my literary agent: Thank you for being all-in from day one.

To my editorial team at Wiley: Your dedication to this project was apparent, and I appreciate each one of you.

To the well-respected authors in the field of conscious leadership who generously provided early endorsements of this book: Thank you for believing in me.

To my best friends: I love our reciprocity and nervous system–resetting hugs, our endless conversations about higher consciousness, and the joy we experience together.

To my chosen family: Each of you brings your unique gifts into my life, and I'm forever grateful for the trust, mutuality, and rootedness of our respective relationships.

To my coaching clients: Your trust, transparency, vulnerability, and willingness to explore this work together made this possible.

To my former agency team: Each of you taught me how to be a better leader.

To my support team in well-being: You all kept me aligned, balanced, and clear—and empowered me to find more compassion, expansion, self-love, and receptivity.

And finally, to my team in spirit for your clarity when working with me and through me on this book.

# About the Author

Kelly L. Campbell (*they/she*) empowers self-aware visionaries to correlate their past wounds to their leadership style, transforming how they lead, live, and love in the world. A certified Trauma-Informed Leadership Coach, Kelly is also an inspiring keynote speaker and the founder of Consciousness Leaders—the world's most diverse and equitable speakers agency. They write for Entrepreneur, have written for Forbes, and offer exclusive content to their Substack community, "THE NEW TLC: Trauma, Leadership, and Consciousness." Early in their career, Kelly was the founder and CEO of a cause marketing agency and sold it in 2016, which led her to advise Fortune 50 corporations, nonprofits, government organizations, and marketing and advertising agencies across the globe. They have hosted two top-rated podcasts since 2006—one on holistic health and wellness and the other on conscious leadership for agency leaders. A longtime conservationist, Kelly was trained by Al Gore as a Climate Reality Leader in 2017. Most recently, she became certified as a Reiki Level III Practitioner. Kelly's vision is to empower more than half of humanity to heal its childhood trauma so that we can reimagine and rebuild the world together.

# Index